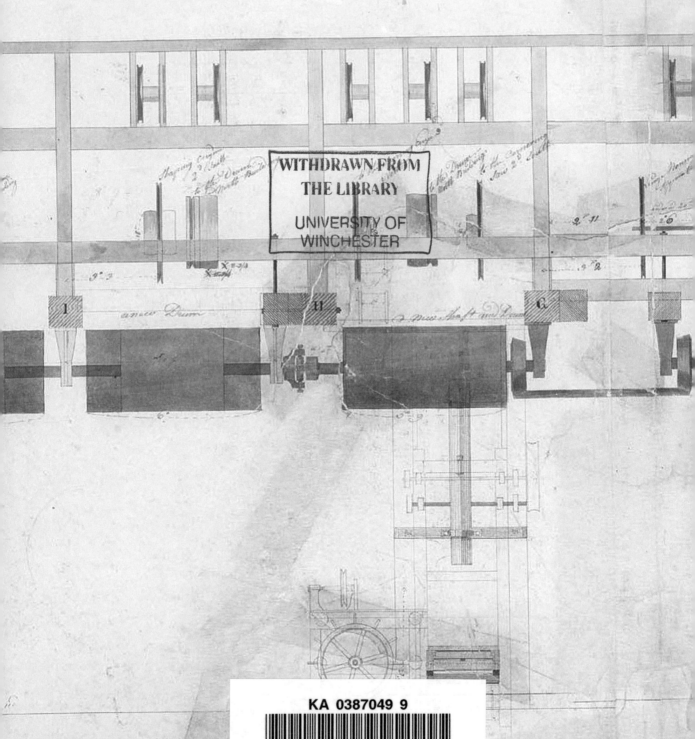

The Portsmouth Block Mills

Bentham, Brunel and the start of the Royal Navy's Industrial Revolution

ENGLISH HERITAGE

Published by English Heritage, Kemble Drive, Swindon SN2 2GZ
www.english-heritage.org.uk
English Heritage is the Government's statutory adviser on all aspects of the
historic environment.

© English Heritage 2005

First published 2005

ISBN 1 873592 87 6

Product code 51035

British Library Cataloguing in Publication data
A CIP catalogue record for this book is available from the British Library.

The National Monuments Record is the public archive of
English Heritage. For more information, contact NMR Enquiry and Research
Services, National Monuments Record Centre, Kemble Drive, Swindon SN2 2GZ;
telephone (01793) 414600.

Brought to publication by Rachel Howard, Publishing, English Heritage,
Kemble Drive, Swindon SN2 2GZ.

Edited by Merle Read
Indexed by Ann Hudson
Page layout by Simon Borrough book design

Printed in England by Bath Press.

Front cover: Looking north across No.1 Basin and dry docks to the Block
Mills. (EH, AA 049687)

Front and back endpapers: Part of a working drawing measuring 51in by
18in (1.3m x 0.46m) dating from around 1805. This shows part of the
arrangement of the overhead line shaft and drums in the roof space of the
central range of the Block Mills, looking North. 'L' is the west wall and 'K' is one
of the cross-beams with a metal hanger supporting the line shaft. To the bottom
left is the large mortising machine; handwritten notes by the drums indicate
which machines they were driving. This is the best evidence for the early layout
of some of the block-making machinery. (Science Museum/Science and Society
Picture Library, GC, C 12)

Title page: The Block Mills from No. 6 Dock. The gabled roof of the northern
range is rebuilding possibly following war damage. (EH, AA 042371)

Back cover: The Block Mills seen from the stern of HMS *Victory,* looking across
No.1 Basin. (EH, AA 049690)

The Portsmouth Block Mills

Bentham, Brunel and the start of the Royal Navy's Industrial Revolution   Jonathan Coad

CONTENTS

FOREWORD

'Indeed, the block machinery at Portsmouth is justly considered one of the wonders of the world'[1]

The Block Mills have long been recognised as one of the seminal buildings of the Industrial Revolution. Indeed, recognition of their significance was immediate – from the very start of their operation in 1803 they attracted huge interest and by 1805 when the final sets of machines were installed they were visited by a procession of the great and the good including Nelson. In June 1814 the Prince Regent, the Emperor Alexander of Russia, the King of Prussia and numerous other German princes visited the Block Mills on their way to review the Fleet. *The Times* recounts how 'All expressed their admiration of the mechanism, which they thought of itself well worth coming to Portsmouth to see.'

This interest was completely warranted. The modest complex of Georgian buildings had witnessed the first use of a steam engine in the Royal Dockyards, the introduction of Samuel Bentham's innovative powered sawmills, the triumphant realisation of Marc Brunel's revolutionary block-making machines and a new order of working practices in the Dockyards. The Block Mills heralded in the age of mass production using machine tools and, accordingly, have received huge attention both in the contemporary technical publications and in modern histories of technology and labour studies. When the Mills finally closed in the 1960s, the Science Museum published a short book extolling the formative influence that their machinery had exerted on the development of the machine tool industry while recent studies have examined their place in the history of mass production and industrialisation of labour.

The emphasis on the technological interest of the machinery has tended somewhat to overshadow the considerable interest of the buildings themselves – a situation that this book seeks to redress. The present day rather mundane surroundings, to the north and east of the Block Mills, mask the hugely historic nature of the site. The buildings are, in fact, located over the former Upper Wet Dock or North Basin. They stand partly on the late 18th-century platform built to house the first horse pumps for draining the water from the neighbouring dry docks and the 1696 Upper Wet Dock and partly on the vaults used to cover over the North Basin in the early 1800s. The survival of these two tiers of vaults, of the platform with its great well and drainage channels and sluices and of the steam engine houses within the South Building is remarkable in itself. When matched to the survival *in situ* of so much of the early transmission system of the block-making machinery and of some of the machines themselves, the Block Mills achieve a significance of the highest order. It is no surprise therefore that upon the cessation of block-making in the 1960s consideration was given to the preservation of the buildings as a museum or guardianship site – a move thwarted by their continued low-key operation use.

The future of the Block Mills is once again under consideration and a recording exercise was undertaken in 2003 by English Heritage to acquaint a new generation with the interest of the buildings and to inform their conservation and proposals for their re-use. This involved archival research, graphical survey of the buildings and the remains of the transmission system and extensive photography of above and below ground features and was combined with an examination of the physical evidence to produce an analytical record of the development of the building archived in the National Monuments Record, Swindon. A summary report was produced for the occasion of the meeting in July 2003 between the Navy and English Heritage to discuss the future of the Block Mills and this led to the recognition that value of this work demanded wider dissemination.

The historical research was therefore greatly expanded in 2004 to provide material for this book. The author, Jonathan Coad, has worked for English Heritage and its predecessor, the Inspectorate of Ancient Monuments for his entire career. He is a Vice-President of the Society for Nautical Research. As the acknowledged expert on the buildings of the Royal Naval Dockyards, he examines anew the primary archival sources, pulls together the major contemporary published accounts and modern commentaries and marries these to the findings of English Heritage's survey work. In this, the Year of the Sea, this book will bring to a new audience the supreme interest of the Block Mills and will underpin the case for their preservation in a fashion commensurate with their importance. English Heritage and the Royal Navy are united by the intent to restore this unique site.

Sir Neil Cossons OBE Chairman, English Heritage

Vice-Admiral Sir James Burnell-Nugent KCB CBE ADC Second Sea Lord and Commander-in-Chief Naval Home Command   **April 2005**

Portsmouth Dockyard. No. 1 Basin, formerly the Great Basin, and the dry docks from the air. This view, looking north-east, shows the Block Mills circled. Beyond lie the buildings of the Victorian dockyard and No. 2 Basin, formerly the Great Steam Basin, constructed in the late 1840s. (EH, NMR 23834/12)

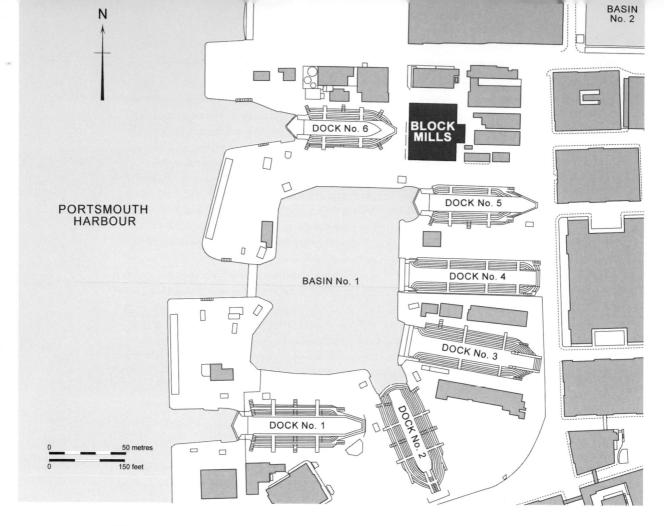

The centre of Portsmouth Dockyard showing No. 1 Basin and the dry docks, with the Block Mills located over the former North Basin. (EH)

PREFACE

The Block Mills in Portsmouth Naval Base have long been known to students of naval and industrial history. Within this group of buildings a remarkable set of machine tools designed by Marc Brunel to manufacture ships' blocks laid the foundations for the subsequent worldwide development of industrial production-lines that used ever more sophisticated machinery to replace the work of individual craftsmen. In a very real sense, the modern world of factory mass-production using machine tools had its origins in this Georgian building overlooking the heart of the dockyard. The importance of the pioneering work in the Block Mills was recognised by discerning contemporaries and the building swiftly became an object of pilgrimage for many, its fame assured by its inclusion in a number of major 19th-century encyclopaedias. Block-making ceased here in 1965, but a number of the machines still survive, in Portsmouth and in the Science Museum in London, while the Block Mills still remain much as completed in the first years of the 19th century, the interiors little altered.

This book has been written to coincide with the bicentenary of the completion of the installation of Brunel's block-making machinery in the spring of 1805. It covers the construction and use of the building and its machinery and aims to set the Block Mills in the wider context of late Georgian dockyard modernisation. Further research in the Goodrich papers has revealed much hitherto unknown information on the crucial early years of this pioneer venture. It is hoped that this book will draw attention to this remarkable building which has stood largely empty for nearly 40 years.

ACKNOWLEDGEMENTS

I first visited the Block Mills in the autumn of 1966, soon after production had ceased here and when all the Brunel machines recently in use were still in place. My guide was the late Robert Sutherland Horne, honorary dockyard historian, enthusiast and mine of information. Through him, I gained my first understanding of this remarkable building, its contents and something of its place in industrial and naval history. Since then, I have come to know the building in much greater detail and have been able to look at many of the original documents relating to its early construction and use. I have benefited enormously from discussions over a number of years with the late Oran Campbell and with Robert Law, architects whose own knowledge and enthusiasm for the building have been crucial in helping to ensure its survival.

This book could not have been written without much help from a number of people. In particular, I owe a debt of gratitude to Tony Woolrich (consultant to English Heritage) for his indefatigable researches in the Goodrich Collection and elsewhere, which have added a great deal of new information. His knowledge of early machinery has also been invaluable. I am especially grateful to him for sharing his knowledge and also for commenting on the text. He has in addition supplied a number of illustrations, added technical information to many of the captions to the machinery and written the appendix on the power transmission. Keith Falconer has masterminded the project with enthusiasm, practical support, knowledge and patience, for which I am most grateful.

In 2003 English Heritage undertook a major survey and appraisal of the evolution of the structure of the Block Mills. Much of the information gained then is incorporated here. Peter Guillery's analysis of the building added considerably to our knowledge. This was greatly helped by the survey drawings by Andrew Donald, George Wilson and Mark Fenton, who also prepared the drawings for this book. The aerial photograph was taken by Damian Grady and the colour photographs were taken by Mike Hesketh-Roberts. The book was brought to publication by Rachel Howard, while Robin Taylor provided support and encouragement. To all these colleagues I am most grateful.

I should also like to thank the staff at the Portsmouth Royal Naval Museum, especially Matthew Sheldon and Victoria Inglis for ferreting out illustrations, as well as the staff of the National Archives, the National Maritime Museum and the Science Museum Library. It is also right to record the benevolent interest of the landlords, a succession of sympathetic flag-officers and their staffs whose priorities, understandably, have to be with the modern fleet and its infrastructure. Last, but far from least, Alec Barlow has generously and willingly shared with me his knowledge and practical experience of block-making and of the last years of production in the Block Mills. Ultimately, however, I take full responsibility for the interpretation and opinions in this book.

Jonathan Coad
Salehurst, Candlemas 2005

PROLOGUE

In the early morning of Saturday 14 September 1805, Admiral Lord Nelson's post-chaise reached the great bastioned land fortifications of Portsmouth after an overnight journey from his home at Merton. After crossing the moat and pausing briefly by the sentries at the Landport Gate, the chaise drew up outside *The George*. It was 6 am. A few hours before, Nelson had seized the opportunity while the horses were being changed at Guildford to write in his private diary: 'Friday night, at half past ten, drove from dear, dear Merton, where I left all which I hold dear in this world, to go to serve my king and country. May the great God whom I adore, enable me to fulfil the expectations of my country.'[1] A fortnight before, news had been brought to his home that the combined Franco-Spanish fleet had been located at Cadiz. On 6 September, Nelson had been given command of the Mediterranean and the Channel fleets, by then blockading the Spanish base. He was to sail as soon as HMS *Victory* could be readied for sea.

HMS *Victory* had been built at Chatham Dockyard and by then was some 40 years old. For four years following

the outbreak of war with Revolutionary France in 1793, she had been at sea as flagship successively for Hood, Man, Linzee and Jervis. Under Sir John Jervis she took part in the Battle of Cape St Vincent in February 1797, but in September she was ordered home to the River Medway for conversion into a hospital ship for prisoners of war. But *Victory* was too valuable as a first-rate, and in 1800 she entered dry dock at Chatham Dockyard for a major refit. This was to be completed in April 1803, only a month before war was renewed with Napoleonic France. Four days after the declaration of war, *Victory* had sailed for the Mediterranean as the flagship of Lord Nelson. For the next two years, *Victory* and Nelson led the blockade of the great French naval base at Toulon, before fruitlessly searching for the French fleet from the eastern Mediterranean to the West Indies and back to Gibraltar. Nelson and *Victory* were then ordered home to Portsmouth, where they arrived on 18 August 1805. While Nelson departed to Merton for well-earned leave, HMS *Victory* was taken in hand by the dockyard for repairs.

It is a tribute to the quality of the 'great repair' at

Figure P.1 The former Naval Academy, established by an Order in Council in 1729 and designed 'for the reception and better educating and training of up to 40 young gentlemen for His Majesty's service at sea...' This was the navy's first purpose-built training establishment. In 1806, it was renamed the Royal Naval College and expanded to accommodate up to 70 cadets. It is now the staff officers' mess. (EH, AA 049708)

Figure P.2 The Commissioner's House and home in 1805 of Sir George Saxton, begun in 1784 to designs by Samuel Wyatt. This is a rare instance of a pre-1795 naval building being designed by a civilian architect rather than by the dockyard officers or the Navy Board's own surveyor. This is the largest of the commissioner's houses, its size reflecting the need to be able to accommodate George III on his visits to inspect the fleet. (EH, AA 049718)

Chatham, and to the resourcefulness of *Victory's* crew in maintaining the warship at sea, that despite the wear and tear of more than two years of almost continuous sea-service, dockyard staff found that only minor repairs were needed. The rigging was overhauled and masts and spars were no doubt checked. By the time Nelson returned to Portsmouth on 14 September, his flagship was refitted, stored and provisioned, and lay at anchor off St Helens.[2]

After breakfasting at *The George*, Nelson set out to call on the 73-year-old Navy Board commissioner Sir George Saxton,[3] who was in charge of the dockyard. His route probably took him through the Portsmouth defences at Quay Gate by the Camber. From there he would have been driven past the fortifications to Beeston's Bastion, across the Mill Dam and through the Mill Redoubt before passing the great Board of Ordnance yard at Gun Wharf. From there, it was a short way to the Hard and through

the main gates of the dockyard. Inside, his carriage would have turned right to pass the Naval Academy (Fig P.1), before arriving outside the Commissioner's House (Fig P.2), now Admiralty House and home of the commander-in-chief, Naval Home Command. The house had only been completed in 1786; Commissioner Saxton had lived there since his appointment three years later. We have no record of the meeting between commissioner and admiral, but after the formal greetings and pleasantries, we know they made a tour of the dockyard. This must have been brief, for Nelson was back at *The George* later that morning. Within the dockyard, contractors were completing the last stages of a huge modernisation and expansion programme; many of the new buildings and docks Nelson would have seen under construction on his earlier visits.

From his house, the commissioner and admiral probably walked down beside the ropery buildings and past the handsome range of new storehouses, today home of the Portsmouth Royal Naval Museum, before reaching the Great Basin and its attendant spread of dry docks (Fig P.3). The last of these had been completed only that year. In number and scale, the dry docks were the largest and most modern set to be found in any European dockyard. They formed the very heart of Portsmouth, focus of a ceaseless hive of activity that was critical to the well-being of the fleet. Much of the routine work undertaken in dry docks was the re-coppering of warship hulls, normally a quick task of a few weeks. The constant patrols and blockade work of the Royal Navy took its toll of copper sheathing, which worked loose and was torn off in severe seas. The 74-gun third-rate HMS *Superb* and the smaller sixth-rate HMS *Squirrel* were then in adjacent dry docks and part-way through their re-coppering. The day before Nelson's visit, the 76-gun HMS *Canada* had been undocked on completion of her resheathing and may well have been secured in the Great Basin. Her place was probably to be taken by the fourth-rate HMS *Europa*, until then lying in the harbour with a leaking hull. This turned out to be a simple repair, in the event taking no more than three days, but two of the other dry docks were occupied long-term by warships undergoing major refits. The 74-gun HMS *Ganges* had been docked in July that year and was to remain in dockyard hands until the following May. Her 10 months in dry dock was short compared to the stay of the smaller fifth-rate, HMS *Ulysses*, which had been docked a year earlier in September 1804 and was not to be undocked until April 1807.[4]

Nelson, with his unending concern for the strength of the fleet, would no doubt have looked with a keen and critical professional eye at all these warships under repair. However, beyond their masts and spars, he could not have failed to notice the tall chimneys of the Wood Mills punctuating the skyline at the northern end of the Great Basin. Housed within them were the Royal Navy's first two steam engines, the earlier of which had begun work in 1799. These powered dock pumps by night and woodworking machinery by day. Although the introduction of steam power to the royal dockyards marked a milestone in their technological development, it was the machine tools that had recently been harnessed to these engines that were causing something of a sensation. Earlier in 1805 the last set of Marc Isambard Brunel's revolutionary machines for making ships' blocks had been installed here. These machines marked the start of the age of mass production using machine tools. Such was to be their fame that it was not long before they gave their name to the whole building. Their introduction, however, had not lacked teething troubles. That September morning, Simon Goodrich was hard at work in the building, thoughts of fame probably far from his mind. As the only engineer employed by the navy, he was responsible for sorting out many of the day-to-day mechanical problems here. His chief concern that morning was the preparation of estimates for a new 30 horsepower engine. All this he noted in his diary. His entry for that day also records, 'Lord Nelson in the Dock Yard. Visits the Wood and Metal Mills.'[5]

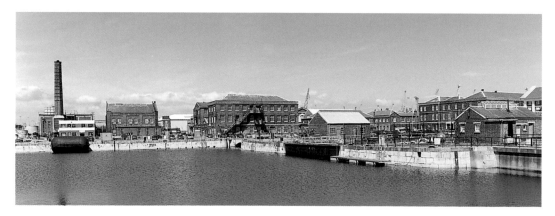

Figure P.3 The Block Mills from across No. 1 Basin. The building was located here to take advantage of the steam engines used for draining the dry-dock system. The dry docks and the basin had evolved in the 18th century from the pioneering work by Edmund Dummer in the 1690s. Today, they form the oldest such group in any European naval base. (EH, AA 042377)

Figure P.4 The Block Mills as viewed from near the stern of HMS *Victory*. At the time of Nelson's visit here in September 1805, the dry docks were a hive of activity as warships were repaired and readied for sea. (EH, AA 042376)

We do not know whether it was Saxton's idea to see the Wood Mills or whether Nelson's natural curiosity was attracted by the smoking chimneys and the novel sounds of mechanical plant at work. Both men would have had reasons for visiting. The commissioner would have wished to impress his distinguished guest with the new factory and its promise of greater dockyard efficiency. Nelson, always keenly interested in the well-being of the Royal Navy, would have wanted to see machinery and a production method that promised so much potential benefit for the fleet. Although he does not mention it, Goodrich probably joined them on their tour to explain the various processes. As the Wood Mills and the Metal Mills stood virtually alone at the northern end of the dockyard, they were probably the last buildings to be visited by Nelson. Before noon, he was back at

The George. Shortly after, he left to make his way through a huge crowd of well-wishers to the shore, where his boat's crew waited to row him out to *Victory*. At 8 am the following morning, 15 September 1805, *Victory* weighed anchor: Trafalgar lay just over a month away (Fig P.4). On board the flagship, although we have no evidence, it seems highly likely that any damaged or worn blocks found in the rigging during her dockyard overhaul would have been made good with replacements from Brunel's new machinery, which Nelson had seen just a few hours earlier. Similarly, *Victory*'s store of blocks would have been likely to have been replenished from the same source. If so, the flagship carried into battle the harbingers of an industrial and technological revolution that within sixty years was to reshape the dockyards yet again and transform the fleet out of all recognition.

13

1 THE ROYAL DOCKYARDS AT THE END OF THE 18TH CENTURY

The introduction of steam power to Portsmouth Dockyard in the last years of the 18th century marked the beginning of a sustained period of innovation and technological revolution within the navy's shore bases. The Royal Navy had perhaps been slow to see the advantages of steam power. However, a combination of circumstances was to ensure that within a very few years, Portsmouth Dockyard was to be in the van of the Industrial Revolution, with a stream of distinguished visitors following in Nelson's wake to the Block Mills.

When war with Revolutionary France broke out in 1793, the Royal Navy was the largest, best equipped and most experienced navy in Europe. A series of maritime wars from the late 17th century, the growth of colonies and the need to protect overseas trade had ensured that most governments throughout the 18th century invested heavily in the fleet. Throughout that century, warships increased both in number and in size. In 1702 the Royal Navy could muster 272 warships with a combined tonnage of nearly 1.6 million tons; at the outbreak of war in 1793 warship numbers had increased to 498 with a combined tonnage of over 4.3 million tons. At the beginning of 1805, ship numbers had soared to 949.[1]

The royal dockyards owe their existence to the establishment of a permanent Royal Navy under the early Tudor monarchs. By the 18th century, the dockyards had clearly defined roles. Although merchants' yards built many of the smaller warships, the royal dockyards held the monopoly for the construction of the larger ships of the line and were responsible for the maintenance and repair of the fleet as a whole. The construction, fitting out and the subsequent maintenance and repair of a warship then, as now, is one of the most complex of all tasks. The concentration of skills and the variety of materials used meant that in pre-industrial England the dockyard towns could lay claim to being probably the most versatile industrial communities in the country. With slow and uncertain inland transport, it made sense to manufacture many of the items within the dockyards. These were both for immediate use and to be stockpiled in dockyard storehouses for warships fitting out for active service or to supply the smaller overseas yards. Other ranges of storehouses were used as lay-apart stores for equipment from ships being put 'in ordinary' or reserve.

The permanent royal dockyards first created by the Tudors tended to be centred on a dry dock. This was for long the single most expensive naval shore installation. Until mechanical pumping was introduced, dry docks had

to be carefully sited to take advantage of the rise and fall of tides to allow gravity drainage. By the outbreak of war with France in 1793, strategic reasons had led to Portsmouth and Plymouth Dock (modern Devonport) becoming the premier home dockyards and fleet bases. Around these two yards were established the great victualling yards, ordnance yards and naval hospitals. Elsewhere, the Navy Board had Woolwich and Deptford yards on the Thames, and Sheerness and Chatham on the Medway. Later in the Napoleonic Wars, Pembroke Yard was to be laid out in south Wales specifically as a shipbuilding yard. The Victualling Board had huge new premises at Deptford, while elsewhere on the Thames the Board of Ordnance stockpiled weapons and gunpowder at the Tower of London, and huge reserves of gunpowder at its new complex at Purfleet on the Essex marshes.

As naval operations began to range further afield on a regular basis, maintenance of the warships, replenishment of their stores and the care of sick and wounded sailors led to the establishment of overseas bases. These began with the capture of Gibraltar in 1704 and Menorca in 1708. The latter remained the navy's most important Mediterranean base for most of the 18th century, and was only supplanted by the capture of Malta in 1800. In the Caribbean, English Harbour, Antigua, and Port Royal, Jamaica gave the navy a permanent presence in the Windward and Leeward Islands. Further north, a naval base was established in 1758 at Halifax, Nova Scotia. By 1795, following the loss of the American colonies with their harbour facilities, a small group of dockyard workers was based at the capital of Bermuda, St George, ultimately transferring to Ireland Island in 1809.[2] Not until the mid-19th century did any of these overseas bases rival any of the home dockyards in terms of size and facilities.

Such was the government investment in the fleet and its shore facilities that by the beginning of George III's reign in 1760, the Royal Navy had grown to be the largest and most complex industrial organisation in the western world.[3] Nevertheless, the Seven Years War was exposing significant deficiencies in the main royal dockyards: the fleet had been expanded but the vital shore facilities had not kept pace. In 1761 the Navy Board, which had responsibility for the dockyards, suggested to the Admiralty that the principal dockyards of Portsmouth and Plymouth should be expanded and modernised to agreed plans. In what must have been one of the most far-sighted and sustained of all government decisions, these proposals were adopted. Such was the extent of the works that they

Figure 1.1 Portsmouth Harbour from the Gun Wharf in 1770. This painting by Dominic Serres shows the harbour mouth with Spithead and the Isle of Wight in the distance. On the Gosport side of the harbour looms the bulk of Haslar Naval Hospital. At the time Serres was painting this tranquil scene, contractors were busy modernising and expanding the dockyard. (© National Maritime Museum, London, BHC 1920)

were to spread over some 40 years and were to be modified on a number of occasions. This timescale was dictated both by the money supply and by the sheer scale of the buildings and engineering works. But it also reflected the absolute necessity of keeping both dockyards fully operational at a time when war or the threats of war were rarely absent. At Portsmouth, additional land for expansion had to be gained by extensive reclamation works in Portsmouth harbour at the northern end of the dockyard. Here, too, the modernisation programme (Fig 1.1) was further affected by two serious fires that laid waste much of the centre of the yard in 1760 and 1770.[4]

At the heart of the modernisation schemes for both Portsmouth and Plymouth was the desire of both Admiralty and Navy Boards for additional and better shore facilities for the growing fleet. More warships demanded more shipbuilding and repair capacity. New building slips and new dry docks were required; extra space was needed to store supplies of timber, and additional saw-pits had to be constructed to process the timber. Wet docks and wharves had to be enlarged. New workshops – smitheries, roperies, mast-houses and sail lofts, treenail makers and block-makers' workshops, rigging houses and paint shops –

all had to be built. As Portsmouth was becoming the central dockyard for fleet maintenance, its need for new facilities, especially dry docks, was urgent (Figs 1.2 and 1.3).

More storehouses were essential, not just to hold reserves of supplies but especially to be available to house equipment from warships returning to be laid up at the end of hostilities. Conscious efforts were made at the start of the rebuilding campaigns to replan both Portsmouth and Plymouth Dock in a logical way to make more efficient use of space and to reduce unnecessary journeys within the yards. Storehouses were constructed near where their contents were needed, and manufacturing activities were centred on the docks and slips. The enormous buildings of the roperies were planned to be sited at the sides of the yards where they would cause least obstruction. A significant element in the modernisation costs stemmed from the desire to build with brick and stone rather than timber. This was not just on grounds of durability but also to contain the spread of fire. Proof of the success of this policy can be seen today with many of these buildings remaining in use more than 200 years later. A number have had their interiors destroyed or damaged, either by accidental fire or by wartime bombing, and in nearly every case the fire was contained within the building concerned. Nobody was more enthusiastic for the dockyard rebuilding programme and nobody was keener to sweep away timber buildings in the dockyards than the Earl of Sandwich, probably the most able of all the 18th-century first lords of the Admiralty; his foresight was to be well justified.[5]

The modernisation programme did not just involve building additional facilities. In many cases, these had to be provided on a far larger scale, a direct consequence of the increasing size of warships. At the end of the 17th century the *Britannia*, a 100-gun first-rate, had a length of 146ft (44.5m) and an extreme breadth of 47ft (14.3m), and displaced 1,620 tons (1,646 metric tons). By the 1780s a 64-gun third-rate had an overall length of 159ft (48.5m) and a breadth of over 44ft (13.4m). By 1800 a 74-gun third-rate displaced nearly 2,000 tons (2,032 metric tons) with dimensions to match, while the newest first-rates comfortably exceeded that figure.[6] The effects were felt throughout the dockyards. More space was needed for timber storage. The master shipwrights needed larger mould lofts to draw out the full-size cross-sections, the shipwrights had to have longer and wider building slips and the sail-makers needed larger sail lofts to spread out the canvas for the principal sails. Mast-makers needed longer mast-houses, and the riggers preparing the fitted rigging needed longer fitted-rigging workshops. Iron fittings grew in number and size. HMS *Victory* carried seven anchors, her two sheet anchors each weighing between 4 and 4$\frac{1}{2}$ tons, the largest iron items to be manufactured in the dockyard smitheries. The 120 fathom (220m) hemp anchor cables, 24in (610mm) in circumference, for these each weighed just over a further 7 tons.[7] Taller masts and longer yards needed more standing and running rigging. New roperies and smitheries inevitably were high on the list of buildings required at both the south-coast yards.

However, the increase in warship sizes had their most immediate and serious effects on the dry docks, where dimensions were crucial. Increased warship lengths could sometimes be accommodated by extending the head of a dock, although this was expensive and time-consuming. Far greater and less tractable problems arose at the entrances to dry docks. These were also the weakest part of the structure and did not lend themselves readily to alterations. Increased warship draughts led to problems with the entrance cills. A partial palliative was to dock and undock only during high spring tides. Another was to lighten a warship by removing all its stores, equipment and guns. The former solution rarely matched the dockyard repair schedule and led to inefficient use of the docks and the warships; the latter was labour-intensive, time-consuming and highly inconvenient. Nevertheless, both remedies, sometimes combined, were increasingly resorted to in the 18th century. The biggest problem of all arose when a warship was too wide for the dry dock. Tinkering with the entrance by rebuilding it might gain a foot or two, but this was never considered practical. The only answer was to rebuild the whole dock on a larger scale.

The pioneering dry docks that Dummer had built at Portsmouth and Plymouth Dock in the 1690s had both been designed to take the first-rate warships of the day. In the case of the Plymouth dry dock, it had an internal length of 230ft (70m) with a width of 49ft (15m) at the gates. The maximum depth over the cill was 22ft (6.7m). This meant that both here and at Portsmouth these docks could cater to a limited extent for the steadily increasing size of the smaller rates, even if the larger rates found themselves gradually excluded.[8] Not surprisingly, the modernisation plans of the 1760s paid especial attention to the provision of new and larger docks, particularly at Portsmouth, where the need was greatest. Here, the first contract for a new dock was let in 1764, but at least a further eight different plans were drawn up between then

Figure 1.2 Portsmouth Harbour and Dockyard, May 1790, by Robert Dodd viewed from the Hard looking north. This gives a good impression of the lively anchorage and some of the new dockyard storehouses on the right. (By permission of the British Library, Maps K Top XIV-49-a)

and 1796 for modernising the docks and slips.[9] Given the 30-year span and the continuing evolution of warship sizes, this is not surprising. However, not only were major civil engineering works involved, but the greater depth of the docks needed for the larger warships led for the first time to a requirement for mechanical pumping on a large scale. Portsmouth was the first British dockyard where this became necessary; elsewhere, tide levels continued to allow drainage by gravity. It was this need for mechanical pumping that ultimately led to the navy's first steam engine being located in the Hampshire yard.

By the early 1790s the reconstruction and enlargement of the two south-coast yards had been under way for some 30 years. In overall charge of the two schemes was the surveyor of the Navy Board in London. His prime task was to oversee warship construction, but he also had a duty to 'examine the plans of all buildings to be erected in any of the dockyards', and to ensure these were built with due attention to durability, utility and economy.[10] In practice the system that had evolved by the mid-18th century saw the surveyor retaining control for the overall layout and planning of the dockyards, consulting his colleagues in the Navy Board and the senior dockyard

Figure 1.3 A rigging hulk and frigate in Portsmouth Harbour, from a painting by E W Cooke. Beyond is the dockyard. The tall semaphore tower on top of the sail loft and rigging house was erected in 1833. (From the author's own collection)

officers, particularly the resident commissioners and the master shipwrights. With the major expansion plans of the 1760s, it is clear that the Admiralty Board also took a close interest, although the dockyards remained the jealously guarded responsibility of the Navy Board. Given the surveyor's workload, it was clearly impossible for him or his assistants to become involved in the detailed design of individual buildings and engineering work. These remained the responsibility of the dockyard officers, principally the commissioner, the master shipwright and his staff. The surveyor wrote letters to these giving general guidance as to what was required. It was then up to the latter to draw the plans and elevations and submit them to the surveyor for approval.

In many respects this system had much to recommend it. It had evolved at a time when the design of buildings was far from the exclusive preserve of professional architects. Builders, tradesmen and the educated classes generally felt themselves well able to draw up their own house plans, or to copy or adapt designs available in the increasing number of pattern books. Similarly, the profession of civil engineer was only in its infancy. Until the 18th century, the term 'engineer' was synonymous with military engineer. Not until 1763 did the term 'civil engineer' appear in a London directory, and it was only in 1771 that the Society of Civil Engineers was founded.[11] Senior officials in the royal dockyards were all practical people who spent their working lives closely involved with warship construction and repair. They probably knew better than anyone else the types and sizes of dockyard structures needed to support these activities. Through long experience, they also acquired knowledge of the effects of local tides and of the geological conditions underneath the dockyards. For Portsmouth dockyard, increasingly making use of reclaimed land, such knowledge was vital when it came to the major civil engineering works associated with new wharves and the dry and wet docks.

The disadvantage of this system was that it asked much of men whose primary tasks were the construction, maintenance and repair of warships. The series of maritime wars in the latter part of the 18th century led to unprecedented burdens on the dockyards and placed increasing pressure on the dockyard staff. It is very much to the credit of these men that the expansion and modernisation programmes for Portsmouth and Plymouth were largely achieved without serious disruption to the efficient support of the fleet.[12] However, there was a price to pay. Inevitably, the horizons of these men tended to be limited to the navy. There is no evidence to indicate that they were aware of developments in the wider world of design and technology outside the dockyard gates.

The major dockyard modernisation plans were getting under way in the 1760s at the very time when Britain as a whole was beginning the shift towards becoming the world's first major industrial nation. Inventions in the textile industry were leading inexorably to the creation of the factory system. John Lombe introduced the first silk-throwing mill at Derby in 1721. This was highly mechanised, and was driven by water power. The first powered cotton mill was constructed in Birmingham in 1741. It depended on donkeys for the motive force, but it was Arkwright's water-powered cotton mill of the 1770s at Cromford in Derbyshire that best epitomised the revolution starting to sweep the textile industry.[13] Industrial expansion, however, was limited as long as it was dependent on water power. In 1712 Newcomen had developed the first practical steam pump for draining mines. In 1746 William Champion had built at Warmley, to the east of Bristol, a fully integrated plant for the manufacture of brass products. The raw materials arrived at one end, and finished goods, such as brass pans, wire and pins, came out the other. The machinery was driven by waterwheels using a large Newcomen engine to recycle the tail-waters, and the machinery included rolling and slitting mills, wire-drawing plant and battery hammers, as well as drop stamps for heading pins. The Newcomen engine had been improved by John Smeaton in the late 1760s, and further improved by James Watt in the 1770s. Watt's engines were used widely for pumping and as blowing engines for the new blast furnaces of the iron-smelting industry. But what industry as a whole needed were steam engines with rotary motions able to transmit power to other machines. In 1783 Watt succeeded in constructing the first such practical steam engine.[14] The rotary steam engine was to liberate industry from its dependence on wind, water, animal or human power.

As most of these developments took place in the mining areas and new industrial towns, far from the dockyards, news of these advances may well have remained largely unknown, or at any rate not appreciated, by dockyard officials and Navy Board alike. Senior naval officers whose country estates lay in these areas must have noticed the changing landscapes, but may not have realised the potential for innovation that industrialisation could bring to their own very different maritime world. However, in 1784 one of James Watt's new steam engines was installed in the Albion flour mills at Blackfriars, where it was to transform the flour-milling industry.[15] Admiralty, Navy and Victualling Boards could scarcely have been unaware of its existence so close to their various offices. Indeed, a few years earlier, around 1781, the Victualling Board approached Matthew Wasborough of Bristol to design a steam engine to power the flour mill at Deptford, using his newly patented crank mechanism. The board also approached John Smeaton, and he urged them to use instead an atmospheric engine to recycle the tail-waters. Nothing seems to have come of these suggestions.

In 1793 war broke out with France. Few then could have foreseen that the struggle would last almost uninterrupted for over 20 years. The size of the armies and navies involved, along with the almost global nature of the conflict, led to unprecedented demands for stores and equipment of all sorts. This in turn provided a huge stimulus for the combatants to devise methods to speed production and to reduce costs. Mechanisation and standardisation were obvious avenues. The invention of the circular saw and its patenting by Samuel Millar of Southampton in 1777 had opened up numerous possibilities in woodworking methods.[16] Similarly, Le Blanc's introduction in France in 1785 of muskets produced with interchangeable parts marked a significant step forward, although not one followed in British arms manufacturing for a number of years. Concurrent with the developments at the Block Mills, mechanisation was to be pursued elsewhere by the navy and military. A steam-powered planing machine for large sizes of timber was installed in Woolwich Arsenal by 1803, and steam-powered vertical saws there and at Chatham were at work before the end of the Napoleonic Wars. Steam-powered saws were also used at Deptford Victualling Yard for cutting barrel staves.

By 1805 a manufactory in London was mass-producing soldiers' water-canteens from wooden parts cut to jigged dimensions by circular saws, the final products needing simple hand-assembly.[17]

With the royal dockyards back on a war footing, attention once again focused on their effectiveness. By then, the great modernisations of Portsmouth and Plymouth were well on the way to completion. The expanded dockyards had been planned with new and spacious facilities. However, these facilities were little different from their predecessors, save in their larger scale. Neither the dockyard records nor the surviving evidence on the ground give much indication that either the Navy Board or the dockyard officers were aware of developments elsewhere. There were no proposals to introduce steam power; the only non-human power was a few horse-gins used for dock pumping and in the roperies. Timber was still laboriously pit-sawn. Despite three serious fires in Portsmouth, it was clear that nobody knew of developments that would lead to the use of cast iron in the buildings and construction of Strutt's fireproof cotton mill at Derby in 1793 and Bage's more celebrated flax mill at Shrewsbury some four years later.[18]

Such criticisms are not wholly fair to either the Navy Board or the dockyard officers. Above all else, the board was concerned with the quality, quantity and reliability of supplies.[19] Early steam plants were expensive and not always reliable. To justify their high cost, they needed to be run regularly and frequently, something not required for dock pumping. Until they were given a rotary motion in 1783, steam engines had only two main uses, as noted: as pumps for mines and as blowing engines for the

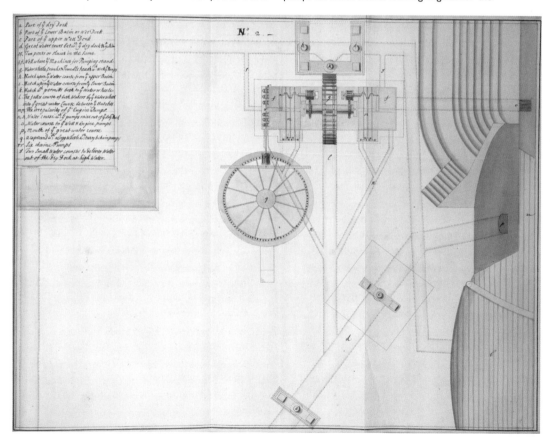

Figure 1.4 Dummer's ingenious arrangement of the 1690s for emptying the new dry dock, part of which is seen to the right. At low tide, the waterwheel was operated by the water held in the wet dock. At other times, the horse-gin provided the power to operated the chain-pumps. (By permission of the British Library, Harleian MS 4318.42)

iron-smelting industry. Pressure for the invention of rotary motion had come principally from the mill owners, increasingly anxious to make their factories independent of the geographical restrictions imposed by reliance on water power. But rotary motion in turn only justified its capital costs if used on a regular and frequent basis – ideal for textile and flour mills, but with less obvious applications in a royal dockyard. Warship-building was essentially a craft industry, requiring a vast number of different shaped parts, all of which had to be formed largely using hand tools. The benefits of steam power would only be realised once it could be linked to machinery that could manufacture standardised items needed in large quantities by the fleet. Given that James Watt had only introduced his rotary motion in 1783, it is at least understandable that over the next few years the dockyards did not find an immediate use for this new source of power.

The Navy Board was not averse to mechanical power where there were clear and practical applications. However, before James Watt's invention, such circumstances were very limited. Nearly 90 years earlier, when Edmund Dummer constructed his dry and wet docks at Portsmouth, he had incorporated an ingenious dock-pumping system for the dry dock, partially powered by a horse-gin and partially by a waterwheel working on the tide-mill principle (Fig 1,4).[20] How long this remained in use is not known, but it seems likely that the waterwheel had been removed by the middle of the 18th century. In 1791 a Mr Seymour suggested the use of a steam engine for the new Chatham ropery, but the understandable fear of fire in such a flammable location led the Navy Board to turn down the idea.[21] It may have been this same fear that led Bentham in the mid-1790s to propose a huge overshot waterwheel to provide power for the Carpenters' and Joiners' Shop at Plymouth Dockyard. The length of the leat necessary for the scheme probably accounted for the idea never getting beyond the drawing board.[22]

The Navy Board was also receptive to ideas for lessening the fire risks in the royal dockyards. Fires in buildings – the driving force behind the development of the use of cast iron that made possible the construction of fireproof mills – remained a perennial concern of the board. One of its great goals for the modernisation schemes at Portsmouth and Plymouth dockyards was to reduce and contain the risk of fire. This was tackled by a policy of demolishing timber buildings and siting those containing hazardous processes, such as the smitheries and tarring houses, at a distance from their neighbours. New structures, where finance permitted, were built using brick or stone for the outer walls, so that any fire would be confined within a particular building. This policy was to be spectacularly vindicated when the Portsmouth and Plymouth roperies burnt. In December 1776 the Portsmouth rope-house was fired by an arsonist and in July 1812 the spinning house at Plymouth caught fire. The interiors of both buildings were gutted, but the fires spread no further. By 1812 the knowledge of construction of fireproof buildings was widespread, and Edward Holl rebuilt the interior of the spinning house using the vocabulary of cast-iron beams, wrought-iron roof members and stone floors. When completed in 1817, its 1200ft (366m) length and three storeys made it one of the largest fireproof buildings in the country.

But in the 1770s such technology did not exist. The interior of the Portsmouth rope-house was restored using traditional timber material.[23] However, when, a few years later, a Mr David Hartley approached the Navy Board with his system of fireproofing buildings, the board was receptive. Hartley's system involved fixing thin iron plates to the undersides of floor boards, to all the exposed surfaces of joists and roof members, and to timber pillars. The board authorised their use in the two new storehouses 'then building' at Portsmouth. These, now 9 and 10 Stores, still retain several areas of the plates. No evidence has yet come to light suggesting any wider application within the dockyards. The Navy Board might have had doubts as to their efficacy   at best the plates would have slowed the spread of fire – or they might not have wanted the disruption of fitting them to buildings already in use. But whatever the reason, their willingness to try the system reflects well on a body often characterised as being over-conservative.[24]

In 1791 the new Society for the Improvement of Naval Architecture was formed: it drew to public attention that 'the French had appointed an Inspector General to maintain their dockyards and assess ship design and alterations'.[25] Such news was not calculated to reassure the more informed sectors of parliament or public opinion. By the mid 1790s, a combination of war, the expansion of European fleets and a growing feeling that the royal dockyards were not in the van of progress were combining to cause mounting anxiety both in government and Admiralty circles. The catalyst for change was to be the arrival at the Admiralty in 1795 of Brigadier General Sir Samuel Bentham to take up the new post of inspector general of naval works.

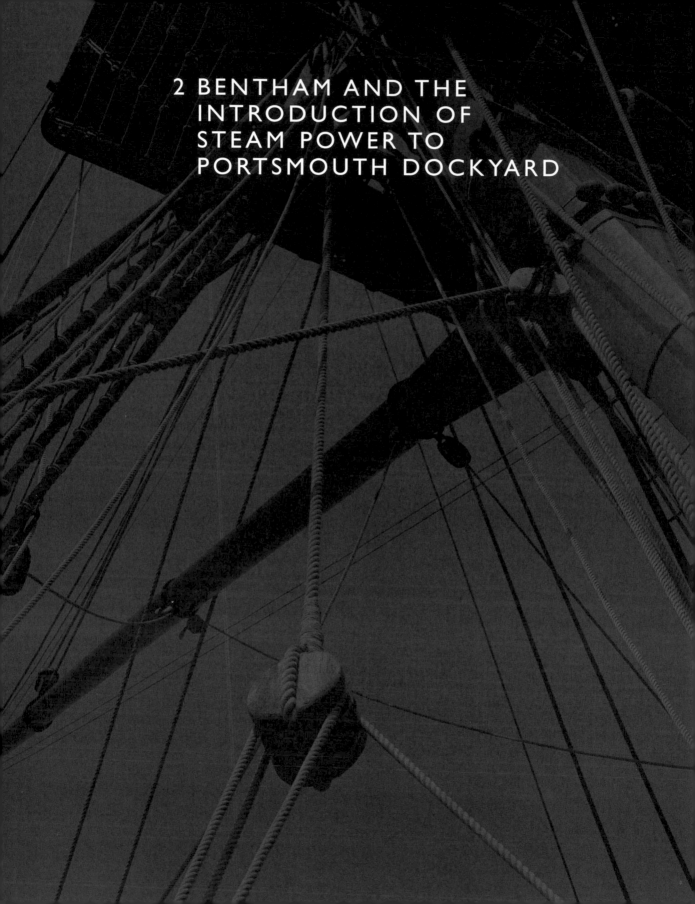

2 BENTHAM AND THE INTRODUCTION OF STEAM POWER TO PORTSMOUTH DOCKYARD

Samuel Bentham took up his new post as inspector general of naval works in April 1795 (Fig 2.1).[1] Less well-known to history than his elder brother, the philosopher Jeremy Bentham, Samuel was then aged 37, with an adventurous career behind him. From boyhood, he had been interested in the navy and in methods of ship construction in the royal dockyards. At the age of 14 he had been apprenticed to the master shipwright at Woolwich before moving to Chatham and then Portsmouth, where he spent two years at the Naval Academy. In 1778 he went to sea for a year with Keppel's fleet. Bentham ascribed his later managerial ideas as to how the dockyards and their workshops should be run to his experience of naval discipline during that time.[2] The following year he set out to tour northern European dockyards before reaching Russia, where he spent the next 12 years. Although commissioned into the Russian army in the service of Empress Catherine the Great, Bentham's interests and talents remained centred on naval shipbuilding and the introduction of more efficient working methods in both industry and agriculture. For a time, he helped construct Prince Potemkin's new Russian navy and ran the base at Kherson on the Dnieper, before managing Potemkin's estate and naval interests at Krichov.[3] He was an early advocate of steam power for manufacturing processes, and his employment gave his inventive mind both the opportunity and scope to devise new forms of wood-working machinery; these machines he patented in England.

In 1791 Samuel returned to England, where he joined his brother, and collaborated in the latter's schemes for penal reform. Central to these proposals was the Panopticon, a prison building with a central hub and wings radiating out like the spokes of a wheel. The original proposal for this design had been Samuel's, and had been intended to revolutionise factory production by allowing supervisors in the central hub to oversee the workmen in the wings. Such a scheme had obvious penal applications, especially when linked to the notion of the inmates in the wings being engaged in productive labour, using machinery. Samuel took on the technical side of the enterprise, developing further his designs for woodworking machinery and touring the principal manufacturing areas to see such machinery as was then in use.

When in Russia, Bentham had invented a wood-planing machine, able to make different profile mouldings by changing the cutter blades. Ten years later, as part of his contribution to the Panopticon project, Samuel designed a range of full-size machines which were erected in outhouses at his brother's house, 19 Queen Square Place, Westminster, London. They were worked by manpower and included veneer-cutting saws, dovetailing and boring machines. They were used for making the parts of sash windows and carriage wheels as a demonstration of their capability. The workmen simply had to assemble the pieces. Bentham took out two patents, No. 1838 in 1791 and No. 1951 in 1793. The first related entirely to planing techniques, using simple gauges and stops to finish timber to a consistent thickness. There is no mention of rotary planers in this patent, but in the second he mentioned planing and edging by this means. Goodrich, writing in November 1804, mentions a rotary planer being at Queen Square Place.[4] The second patent is more comprehensive, and, among other topics, includes very detailed notes for the use of the circular saw in joinery production, the use of rotary cutters to make dovetails and the use of rotary cutters, the circular saw and reciprocating chisels for making mortises and tenons. There are features in this patent which were later to appear in Brunel's block-making machines (see chapter 4, note 6).

Bentham's various inventions led to his being described as 'the father of woodworking machinery',[5] and his patents as 'truly remarkable examples of inventive genius . . . in the specifications the principles involved in many of the most important machines in present use are claimed and set forth in the clearest possible manner'.[6] The fame of his machines attracted many visitors, including Henry Dundas Secretary at War, later Lord Melville and First Lord of the Admiralty, who praised them in speeches to the House of Commons. Bentham was visited by Earl Spencer and the Commissioners of the Admiralty, who saw the advantages of Bentham's ideas. Clearly his demonstration and reputation were crucial to his appointment as inspector general.

Although the Benthams had little success with the penal project, the period of three years Samuel spent on this work no doubt enabled him to absorb his brother's utilitarian philosophy, which was to have such a powerful effect on Victorian thinking. It also allowed Samuel time to develop his own ideas on the efficient running of the dockyards, and enabled him to present a powerful case for modernising and mechanising the latter when he approached the Board of Admiralty early in 1795.[7]

Samuel Bentham could not have chosen a more propitious time to advance his ideas. Both the First Lord, Earl Spencer, and Charles Middleton, later Lord Barham, were enthusiasts for dockyard modernisation and reform. Earl Spencer himself was a personal friend of Bentham.[8] In the latter's papers are a series of undated drafts addressed to George III outlining the need for a new department to modernise warship construction methods and to improve dockyard efficiency. These drafts were drawn up by the Board of Admiralty, but are clearly influenced by Samuel. They represent possibly the earliest attempt to apply scientific principles to the organisation and running of the royal dockyards.

The draft proposed the establishment of an inspector general of naval works at the head of a small department that would include the first salaried architect, who would also combine the role of a structural engineer, a mechanist or mechanical engineer, and a chemist whose principal task was to be the examination of 'the causes of decay in all bodies and the means of preventing it [and] . . . to devise means of securing ships from fire'.[9]

These proposals were accepted, and the new department was established with Samuel Bentham at its head. Traditionally, the organisation and running of the royal dockyards were strictly the business of the Navy Board. It is a reflection of Admiralty concern about the way its sister board was discharging these duties that the Admiralty was prepared to risk the resentment of the latter board by muscling in on its territory. Over the next years, this was to be the cause of much friction. On 22 April 1795 the Admiralty instructed Bentham to visit all the home dockyards to see how their operations might be improved. The same day, it wrote to the Navy Board requesting free access to the yards for the inspector general of naval works. The letter clearly spelt out the reasons for his appointment:

Having taken into our consideration the general state of the present practice in relation to the several branches of business carried out in His Majesty's Dockyards, and observing how little advantage appears to have been hitherto taken of a variety of improvements, particularly in the application of mechanical powers, that modern discoveries have brought to light, and having taken a view of a system of machinery combined and carried into practice by Brigadier General Bentham, which appears to be capable of being adapted with peculiar advantage to various works carried on in the said dockyards, we are induced to take such measures as may procure to His Majesty's service, the benefits of Brigadier Bentham's ingenuity and experience as well in England as in foreign countries.[10]

Bentham wasted no time. Within six weeks he had visited Portsmouth and drawn up a plan to reorganise radically the layout and design of the dry docks then under construction. These proposals were sent by the Admiralty to the Navy Board for its consideration in early June 1795. The accompanying letter stated baldly that the 'nature [of the plan] the General will explain to you at any time you may appoint'. The next sentence was a firm order to stop all works on the dry docks.[11] Such peremptory instructions no doubt realised the worst fears of the Navy Board about Bentham's new department. Despite vigorous opposition to his proposals from the Portsmouth Dockyard officers, in October the Admiralty instructed the Navy Board to proceed with the general's scheme, as set out in June. It was to cost an additional £152,000.[12]

The reasons for Bentham focusing on Portsmouth Dockyard are not far to seek. By then, it was by far and away the navy's largest refitting yard, where any delays in work schedules could have an immediate impact on the effectiveness of the fleet.[13] Minor refits could be undertaken with the warships remaining afloat, but for any work involving significant repairs to the hulls, dry docks were essential. The latter all too often were the limiting factor in a dockyard's efficiency; there is also strong evidence that in the early part of the Napoleonic Wars the Portsmouth dry docks were the cause of significant problems.[14] It was these problems that first engaged Bentham's attention, but also gave him the chance to assess the dockyard's potential for making radical improvements in efficiency and output by introducing steam power and his woodworking machinery. A further bonus was Portsmouth's proximity to Redbridge, where Bentham was closely involved between 1796 and 1798 with the shipbuilding firm of Hobbs and Hellyer. They were to build six experimental ships to Bentham's designs

Figure 2.2 Two of the reciprocating saws designed by Samuel Bentham. The Sadler steam engine on the right suggests that this is a design for the proposed installation at Redbridge. (University College, London, cxvii.24)

and were also apparently willing to experiment with the use of some of Bentham's machinery[15] (Fig 2.2).

At Portsmouth, Bentham was to find the Royal Navy's largest concentration of dry docks. These were centred on the Great Basin, or wet dock, where warships could be held afloat at a constant level. Although a very few primitive dry docks were apparently in use by the late 15th century, modern dry docks owe much to the pioneering work of Edmund Dummer at Portsmouth and Plymouth in the 1690s.[16] At Portsmouth he constructed the Great Basin, later extended south and now known as No. 1 Basin. Opening off the northern end of its east side was one of the two earliest stepped dry docks in Great Britain. This, his Great Stone Dock of 1690, was extensively reconstructed in 1769 and is now No. 5 Dock. North of the Great Basin, and approached originally from the harbour by a stone-lined channel, Dummer constructed a second rectangular wet dock known as the Upper Wet Dock or North Basin. In 1699, by placing gates at both ends of the approach channel, Dummer was able to create a second dry dock, although one that lacked the innovative stepped sides of the Great Stone Dock. This second dry dock was rebuilt in 1737 with stepped sides and a stone

eastern head, and was renamed the North Stone Dock, now No. 6 Dock. This reconstruction left the North Basin inaccessible to ships and effectively redundant for its original purpose.[17]

By the middle of the 18th century, although the dry-dock system at Portsmouth was more extensive and elaborate than at any other naval base, it was proving inadequate. The one double and two single dry docks were too few in number for the size of the fleet and were becoming too small for the larger classes of warships then coming into service. The Great Basin, too, was inadequate, and was further encumbered by a slip on its east side. The modernisation plans of 1764 envisaged the construction of a further dry dock – now No. 4 dock – to replace the slip and the enlargement of the existing dry docks. As early as 1761 an imaginative scheme had been proposed to link all the drainage culverts from the existing dry docks to the redundant North Basin, and to deepen the latter and use it as a huge sump into which the dry docks could drain by gravity.[18] The collected water could then be pumped into the harbour at leisure by horse-gins (Fig 2.3). Work on this remarkable drainage scheme got under way in 1771, and – with the ultimate exception of the distant No. 1 Dock,

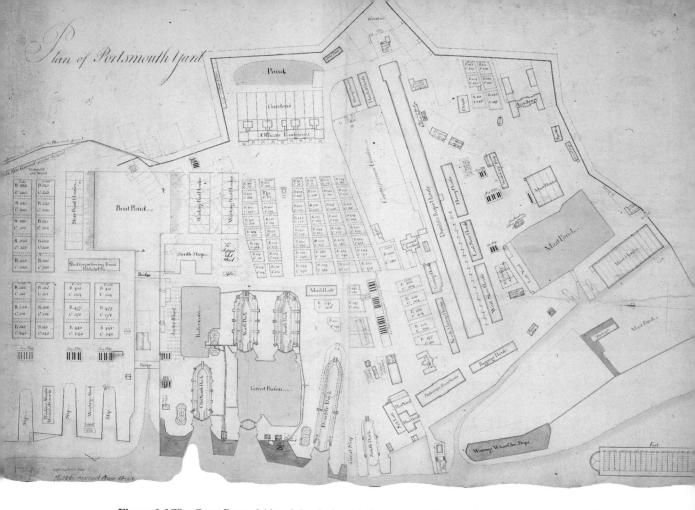

Figure 2.3 The Great Bason [*sic*] and dry docks with the new centralised drainage scheme as proposed in 1770. Right of the Great Basin is the double dock. (The National Archives (PRO), ADM 140/555, 5)

which was given its own set of horse pumps – all future new dry docks around the basin were linked to the system.[19] By around 1776 all these drainage works had apparently been completed, the old North Basin had been deepened and renamed the reservoir, and for the next nine years the contractors were busy elsewhere in the dockyard. When this new system of centralised drainage was first in use, it marked an important step forward in the efficient use of the dry docks. The capacity of the old North Basin as a sump allowed time for the horse-gins to empty the water into the harbour. By a coincidence, this scheme was being installed at the same time as the Spanish navy was installing a steam engine to pump out its dry dock at Cartagena. This was very probably the first steam engine in any European dockyard, its use here a reflection of the difficult problems faced by Spanish engineers in a tideless Mediterranean.[20]

But by the 1780s the Portsmouth dry docks were again proving inadequate in number. Fresh plans of improvement were drawn up in 1785; these were revised the following year and again in 1788. Indecision centred on the future of the existing double dock that lay just to the south of the Great Basin. The former was in need of repair or replacement; until its future was decided it was difficult to plan other works in its vicinity. By then, there were mixed views on the merits of double docks. Although they took up less space at the waterfront, this benefit was felt to be outweighed by inefficiencies resulting from any failures to synchronise closely the repair times of warships using them. While this debate continued, the only progress that could be made was to construct a much larger single dock to the south of the double dock. This, now No. 1 Dock, was begun in 1789 and was completed in 1795.

Shortly before Bentham's arrival at the Admiralty, the Navy Board took the decision to replace the double dock with a new double dock, and in February 1795 let a contract with the principal dockyard contractor, Thomas and John Parlby.[21] Ground works were just starting as Bentham took up his appointment; it was these he promptly halted in June and replaced by a wholly new scheme of his own. Bentham proposed to extend the Great Basin southwards, over the site of the double dock, and to build two new dry docks (now Nos 2 and 3 docks) projecting east and south-east from the south-east corner of the extended basin. In 1796 work began on enlarging the Great Basin, and by 1799 it had proceeded to the point where work could begin on the two dry docks. When these works were completed in 1805, the complex of dry docks had assumed the configuration that exists today. One of these new dry docks, No. 2 Dock, is home to HMS Victory; collectively, the complex is the oldest such set in the world (Fig 2.4).[22]

Construction of dry and wet docks involved very major civil engineering, no more so than at Portsmouth, where the lack of firm subsoil had long been a problem. Up until Bentham's arrival, the Portsmouth dry docks had been constructed with masonry walls and timber floors underpinned by timber piles. The floors and walls were not firmly tied to each other. This meant that the gate piers themselves were not linked to each other by any direct means. This was a potentially serious structural weakness, for the dock gates and piers on which they were hung had to withstand the full force of each high tide. The waterproof fit of the dock gates depended on the absolute immovability of the gate piers. In the 18th century various attempts were made at Portsmouth to mitigate this weakness with extensive piling, but the problem persisted and became more acute as warships grew larger and heavier, and dry docks became wider and deeper. Bentham's elegant solution was to replace the timber floor at the dock entrance with an inverted masonry arch that firmly linked the gate piers and lessened the need for piling. His two new dry docks were built on this principle; the records are unclear, but it is possible that the whole of the dock floors were tied to the inverted arches and not just the areas round each entrance.

Bentham's next contribution to dock design was the development of the caisson. In 1703 Commissioner St Lo at Chatham had constructed a prototype caisson and

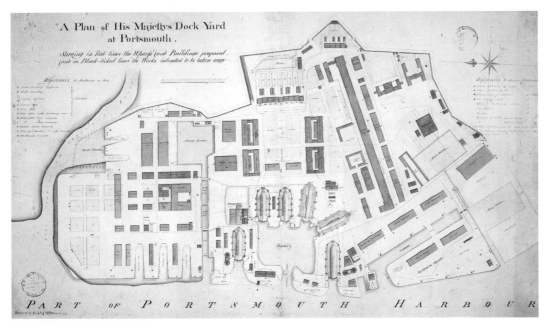

Figure 2.4 The Great Basin and dry docks as they had finally evolved by 1805. This plan clearly shows the new Wood Mills over the reservoir and the elaborate culvert system. The thin lines represent Bentham's new piped water system. The two engine houses can be seen encapsulated within the south range of the Wood Mills. (The National Archives (PRO), ADM 140/555, 17)

although the dockyard officers liked it, nothing more was heard of it. It is unlikely that Bentham was aware of St Lo's invention. In 1798 Bentham proposed a 'hollow floating dam' or caisson for the entrance to the enlarged Great Basin, and one was built for this in 1802. The great advantage was its width, which allowed wagons and carriages to cross over it, thus saving a very considerable detour.[23]

These major engineering works took up much of Bentham's time during his first years. However, the centralised arrangements for draining the Portsmouth dry docks by gravity into the reservoir also gave him a unique and ready-made installation where he could evaluate the potential for introducing steam power in a royal dockyard. The 1770s scheme that had turned the old North Basin into a giant sump ultimately depended on horse pumps to lift the water into the harbour. These pumps had been constructed on a rectangular masonry base projecting out into the reservoir towards the western end of its south side. The two horse-gins were linked to a battery of 16-chain pumps in a huge hexagonal stone-lined well shaft set a little to the south between the gins. This arrangement appears to have worked well for the next quarter of a century. However, as Bentham noted in December 1797, the additional dry docks then under construction (Nos 2 and 3) and the deepening of the Great Basin would be beyond the pumps' capacity.[24]

This system, though, was already on a scale that made the substitution of steam power well worth considering, especially now that Watt had given steam engines a simple and effective rotary motion. An individual dry dock might only need to be pumped dry every few months. Where

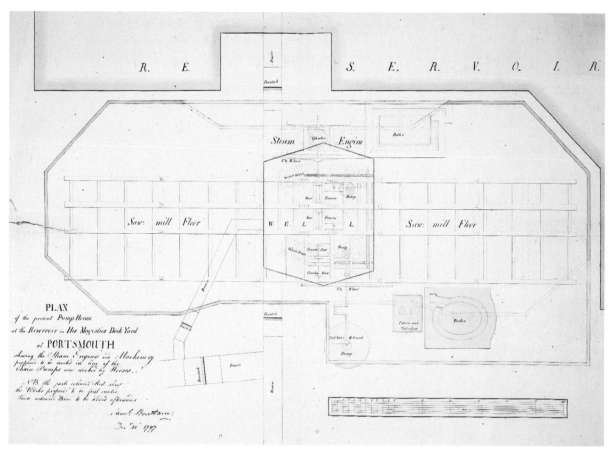

Figure 2.5 Bentham's 1797 proposals for the steam engine linked to the existing horse-powered pumping system. In this scheme, which was not implemented, Bentham has incorporated a sawmill above the horse-gin and pumps. (The National Archives (PRO), ADM 140/495)

Figure 2.6 'Elevation of Mr Sadler's Steam Engine showing the Boiler and Flywheel'. A drawing signed by Samuel Bentham on 21 December 1797. (The National Archives (PRO), ADM 140/496, No. 2)

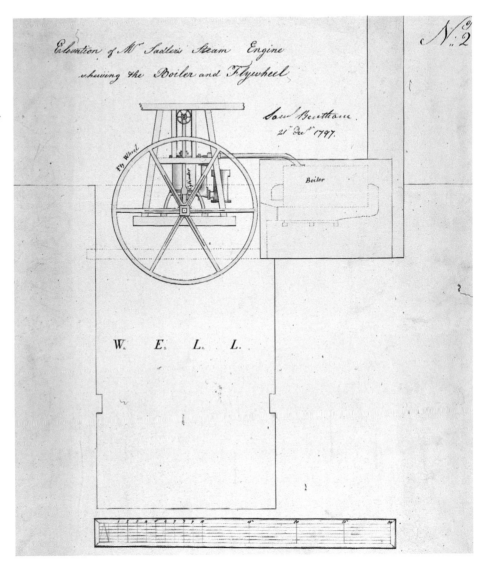

horses provided the motive power for pumps, they could easily be deployed to other dockyard tasks, such as hauling wagons or dragging timber. The capital expense of a steam engine dedicated just to empty one dry dock could never be justified purely in economic terms. At Portsmouth, the economies of scale resulting from the sophisticated common drainage system made the case for steam far more attractive. It became overwhelmingly so when Bentham proposed to make the steam engine the central motive power for a whole variety of tasks.

By the end of 1797 Bentham's hopes of introducing his machinery at Hobbs and Hellyer's yard at Redbridge were fading. He had commissioned a steam engine for the shipyard to a design by James Sadler, the chemist on his staff, but problems with apparent patent infringements had prevented its use there. With his experimental vessels already well under construction, the time was rapidly passing when it would be worth setting up his woodworking machinery at the shipyard.[25] Instead, he suggested in a letter to Evan Nepean, secretary to the Admiralty, a far more ambitious proposal for Portsmouth. This really marked the start of the steam age in the royal dockyards, many years before steam propulsion was used in a naval vessel (Figs 2.5, 2.6 and 2.7).

29

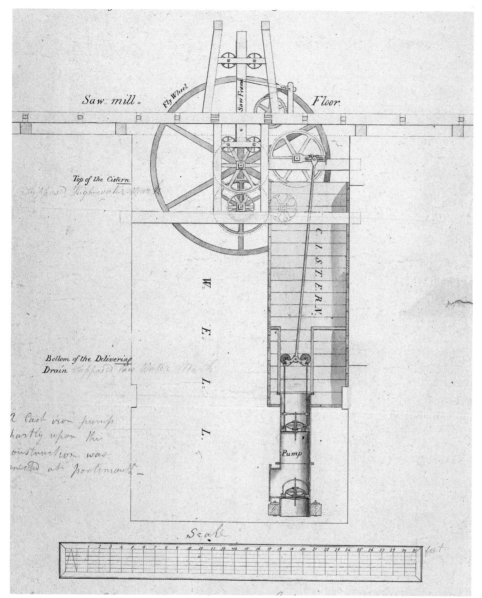

Saw_mill =   Fly Wheel.   Saw Frame   Floor.

Top of the Cistern.

Suffos.? highwater Mark

C. I. S. T. E. R. N.

W =
E =
L =
L.

Bottom of the Delivering
Drain *Suffosed Low Water Mark*

*a cast iron pump
partly upon this
construction was
erected at Portsmouth* —

Pump

Scale

1 2 3 4 5 6 7 8 9 10 11 12 13 14 15 16 17 18 19 20 feet

Figure 2.7 A 1797 drawing showing Bentham's proposals for machinery for pumping and sawing. There is no evidence that this particular scheme was ever built. (The National Archives (PRO), ADM 140/496, No. 3)

Bentham's proposals amounted to a complete package of tasks, all of which would be powered by Sadler's engine 'that was now available and could be delivered to Portsmouth'.[26] Key to the economy and utility of the scheme was his plan to use the engine at night to pump the reservoir and by day to power a variety of his woodworking machines. Not many precise details are known about Bentham's woodworking machinery, but his 1797 proposals are presumably based on his earlier patents.[27] These centred on methods for planing, sawing using reciprocating blades, mortising, milling, boring and the use of lathes. There was also a proposal for using steam for bending timber. In his letter to Nepean, Bentham envisaged reciprocating saws being used for 'sawing in general, particularly straight work, such as siding of timbers, slitting Deals, cutting, quartering straight planks of all kind'. Using the steam engine's rotary motion, he planned tonguing and grooving, rebating and 'cross-cutting into lengths Deals of all sorts for joiners and house carpenters' work'.[28]

Unlike the later Maudslay-manufactured Brunel machinery with its rigid iron frames, all the Bentham machines were built with timber frames which inevitably limited the longevity of the machines and their degree of accuracy. Bentham was convinced that capital costs were now favouring steam power: he reported that horse pumps installed for the recently completed South Dock (now No. I Dock) had cost £2,758, whereas he estimated that a steam engine 'of Mr Sadler's construction' would cost £800, pumping apparatus £500 and sawing machinery £600. This proposal also incorporated a small freshwater well adjacent to the main chain pumps. This well may have been used principally to provide a supply of fresh water for the engine boilers, but it also supplied two lead-lined timber framed cisterns that each held some 45 tons of water. These were described in 1817 as being 'just above the level of the yard and thus saving the expense of power in raising this water up to the higher level of the [later] Cisterns over the Wood Mills'. As such, they continued in use long after the much larger cisterns. By 1817 one cistern frame was rotten and had to be demolished, but it was thought worthwhile to enlarge the remaining one to hold 75 tons of water.[29]

By April 1798, when Bentham wrote to his half-brother Charles Abbot, chairman of the Select Committee on Finance, he had further refined and extended his proposals. The steam engine was now to power extra pumps in a freshwater well 'for supplying the fleet in harbour, and for extinguishing fires in any part of the dockyard'.[30] This well (see Fig 2.13) was to be the source of potable water supplied by a system of cast-iron water mains laid round the dockyard and pressured from large storage tanks on the roofs of the new Wood Mills. Ultimately, this system also incorporated in some dockyard buildings what may well have been the pioneer sprinkler system for fire-fighting.[31] Bentham's faith in the ability and durability of one steam engine to continue to work all this different apparatus was a little optimistic, and over the next few years new and more powerful engines had to be added to the system. It must also be remembered that in the late 1790s steam power introduced a wholly new technology to dockyards that initially lacked the skills and equipment to provide the necessary support. When Sadler's engine fractured a piston rod a few months after installation, a pattern had to be made and sent to London, as nobody in the

Figure 2.8 The interior of the single-storey engine house built to contain Sadler's steam engine. The building was slightly adapted to house replacement engines in 1807 and 1830. This space marks the heart of the Royal Navy's first use of steam power. (EH, AA 042399)

dockyard had either the experience or facilities to manufacture a new one.[32]

On 19 April 1798 the Admiralty ordered the Navy Board to proceed with Bentham's proposals for the introduction of steam power at the Hampshire dockyard.[33] At its centre was Sadler's engine, which began pumping work in March 1799. Drawings of the machine show it to have been a very early table engine, an invention usually credited to Henry Maudslay.[34] The Sadler engine was housed in a rectangular single-storey brick engine-house, replacing the eastern of the two horse-gins (Fig 2.8).

Although the records are not clear, this engine was probably harnessed the following year to a new and larger pair of chain pumps. An undated drawing in the Goodrich Collection shows just such a set, each pump tube having a diameter of 2ft (610mm). They were arranged in two sets of three and raised water from depth of around 20ft (6m) in two lifts.[35] Either set could be run independently of the other by altering the gearing from the engine, These may be the set of pumps made by Collins and Broughton at a cost of £792 13s 8d and delivered to the site in 1800.[36] The western horse-gin meanwhile remained in position as emergency back-up.

The restricted site of the pumps, horse-gin and new engine-house meant that there was apparently no space for any of Bentham's woodworking machines. Although sawing machinery had been included in the December 1797 estimate, with a plan showing a sawmill incorporated at a higher level over the top of the chain pumps (see Fig 2.5), this sawmill does not seem to have been built.[37]

The Sadler engine initially was probably limited to pumping. Nevertheless, by October 1799, Bentham was strongly advocating the addition of a second steam engine of 30hp to guard against mechanical failure and allow the complete removal of the horse pumps. He noted that the leaky state of the basin gates was making the pump ineffectual. He also envisaged a further task for both engines, and one that reflects the increasing inability of the existing dry docks to cope with newer and larger warships with their greater displacements. Bentham reckoned that the increased capacity of the two engines would allow them to *raise* the water level in the Great Basin to give greater depth of water over the cills of the dry docks so that 'even with regard to the old docks in the Basin, not more than the delay of a day need take place for want of water whether Neap or Spring tides for the undocking or docking of ships of the largest size, or for placing them on chocks of the most convenient height'.[38]

At the beginning of February 1800 Bentham wrote again to Nepean, urging purchase of an engine (Fig 2.9). His letter conveys something of the flavour of these pioneering days of steam power:

I would propose in consideration of the well-established reputation of the steam engines manufactured by Messrs Boulton and Watt and the superior means which these gentlemen have of ensuring accuracy and sufficiency in the workmanship of this article of machinery as well as despatch in the execution of it, that the Navy Board be directed to agree with Messrs Boulton and Watt for the delivery at Portsmouth as soon as possible of all the parts usually furnished by them of a steam engine of their construction and for sending a man of their choice to direct the putting it up as is usual when they furnish steam engines to private individuals. . . . The sort of steam engine for which the machinery intended for Portsmouth is adapted is a double stroke engine the cylinder of which is twenty eight and a half inches in diameter, the length of the stroke six feet, and to work with a crank.

Bentham helpfully added that 'Messrs Boulton and Watt are at present in town and their direction is at Mrs Matthew's London Street, Fenchurch Street'.[39] His letter had the desired effect, for on 17 February the Admiralty ordered the Navy Board to 'treat with Messrs Boulton and Watt for the Machinery . . . that it may be delivered to Portsmouth as soon as possible'.[40] In October the Navy Board was able to inform the Portsmouth officers that Boulton and Watt had 'shipped the materials of the steam engine [from] Bristol on board the *Pheasant* for your yard'. The yard officers were instructed to 'endeavour to have a proper person in readiness to erect the same as soon as they are apprised of his being wanted'.[41] The beam engine was the standard Boulton and Watt design of double-acting engine, with a timber beam 20ft 6in (6.25m) long. The flywheel was 21ft (6.4m) in diameter. As with all such engines then, final construction details were left to the engine erectors on site.[42]

Despite Bentham's high opinion of the workmanship of Boulton and Watt, part of the iron boiler that arrived with the engine was found 'deficient'.[43] It would seem that the problem remained unresolved. In January 1801 a scale model of a boiler was sent to the dockyard to be used to instruct the millwrights as to how the boiler should be assembled, but this apparently did not help.[44] A year later a new boiler was ordered from Booth, Littlewood & Co of Sheffield; this was delivered to Deptford Dockyard in August 1802 for onward shipping to Portsmouth.[45]

Surviving plans and drawings of the Boulton and Watt engine house show a narrow three-storey building located in line and to the west of the Sadler engine house, with a small two-storey boiler house on its southern side. The drawings are typical of engine houses of the period where the designs were provided by the engine manufacturers. It is probable that the new engine was completed and working by the spring of 1801, although the problems with the boilers were to drag on for over a year. In 1802, when

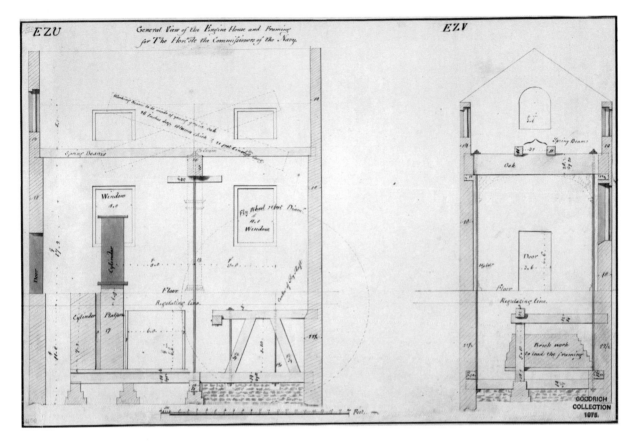

Figure 2.9 Boulton and Watt's 1800 proposal for an engine house for the Royal Navy's second engine. An engine house of this type was constructed, and part remains embedded within the western end of the south range of the Wood Mills. (Science Museum/Science and Society Picture Library, GC, C 15)

Bentham received permission to construct the Wood Mills, both existing boiler houses – along with the Sadler engine house and the new Boulton and Watt engine house – were to be subsumed in the south range of this new building. In April 1802 Bentham reckoned that the vaults in the North Basin were sufficiently advanced for construction of the Wood Mills to be started.[46] The shells of both engine houses remain substantially intact within the south range today. An examination of the external fabric of the north side of the south range shows no obvious joints between it and the brickwork of the north wall of the Boulton and Watt engine house. However, the rhythm of the ground- and first-floor windows on the north side of the south range, together with the survival to second-floor height of the east wall of the engine house, with its now-redundant first-floor window, provides the strongest physical evidence for the phased

construction of this range. The documentary evidence indicates that the Boulton and Watt engine and boiler house must have been free-standing, probably for the best part of 18 months.[47]

It is apparent that over the first few years there were various suggestions made as to the best fuel for the boilers. An undated cross-section shows a pair of wagon boilers with a note in the margin indicating that the bars of one of the boilers were to be of dimensions suitable for burning wood – an ideal way of making use of the endless free supply of offcuts available in the dockyard.[48] Goodrich also suggested that the boiler firebox should be capable of burning 'cinders from the smiths' forges of which . . . a great deal is thrown away by the Dock Yard'. Conscious that the clinkers from cinders could quickly choke the firebox, Goodrich added that it would be sensible to consult Boulton and Watt, who 'may have some experience

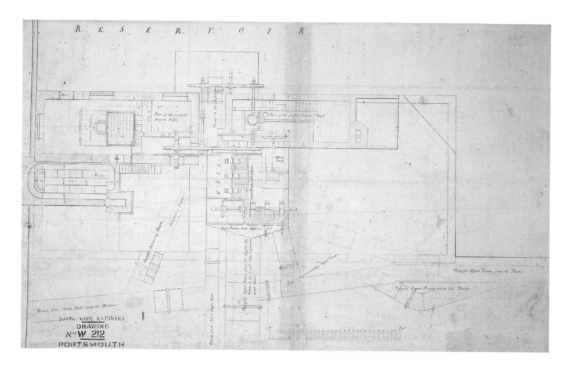

Figure 2.10 A plan of *c*1800 showing the chain pumps and the existing Sadler engine house. The 'proposed' Boulton and Watt engine house is to the left. The limited space available on the horse-gin platform is at once apparent. The still-uncovered reservoir is at the top of the plan. (The National Archives (PRO), Works 41/381)

of burning cinders from Smiths' forges [and] may know best how to construct a fireplace to suit them'.[49] Boulton and Watt replied rather huffily that they 'had no experience of the burning of cinders under the boilers of steam engines, and very little of burning of wood'. They added that it was likely that the grate area would need to be considerably larger.[50] By 1808 Brunel noted that the Block Mills were using 1 chaldron (approximately 2 tons) of coal each day and that 'no wood is used at present'.[51] It is probable that, by then, experience had shown that the greater calorific value of coal was essential to maintain sufficient heads of steam in the various boilers.

In January that year Bentham decided that he had to visit the works at Portsmouth with some of his staff. In his letter to the First Lord of the Admiralty, he noted that 'the work requisite for the completion of the Basins and Docks, and for the erection of the machinery at Portsmouth is going on with a degree of alacrity far beyond what I have ever known before in a dockyard'. Nevertheless he felt that 'there seems reason to believe that those works might go on better still were I to go

there myself'[52] (Fig 2.10). The inspector general was a firm believer in seeing for himself, although he does not record in this instance whether or not his presence helped expedite matters.

Although the new engine house and its machinery would have taken up part of Bentham's time in the dockyard, the new freshwater well was an equally impressive part of his modernisation plans. Until then Portsmouth Dockyard had drawn its supplies from a number of wells, but these had limited capacity and were inconveniently located for supplying the warships. Instead, the latter normally had to cross the harbour to take on water at the Weevil Victualling Yard. In 1797 Bentham had looked at the possibilities of laying a dockyard water main. Such a system was only possible if a secure and copious source of fresh water could be located. In September the following year, Bentham authorised the sinking of a very substantial well some 400ft (122m) to the south-east of the steam engines and near the Joiners' Shop. The well chamber at the head was constructed with a diameter of 25ft (7.6m); the well shaft itself had a diameter of 5ft

Figure 2.11 Detail of the two batteries of chain pumps and the drives from the steam engines. The pumps acted in two lifts, each pump raising about 10 tons of water a minute. The cranked shaft leading diagonally off the spur wheel was linked to the new freshwater well, where it powered the pump. (Science Museum/Science and Society Picture Library, GC, C 102)

(1.5m) and was excavated to a depth of 104ft (32m). Goodrich records that the well diggers had to contend with gravel, 'running muddy sand', a stratum of blue clay at a depth of 49ft (15m) and the constant ingress of salt water. At the bottom of the well shaft, two copper pipes of 3in (76mm) and 4in (102mm) bores were driven to a depth of 274ft (83.5m) from the surface. At this point, fresh spring-water was discovered in quantities that would allow some 520 tons (528 metric tons) to be pumped every 24 hours. The well pumps themselves were powered by a horizontal rod connected by a crank to the steam engines at the other end of the brick-vaulted tunnel built to link the two installations (Figs 2.11 and 2.12). The excavation of the well was a major engineering enterprise, directly comparable in scale to the two great contemporary wells sunk by the Royal Engineers at Dover within the castle and the fortifications on Western Heights.[53] However, the Portsmouth well (Fig 2.13) was not an unqualified success. It was to suffer from problems of silting and diminishing flow, and in the mid-1820s

Goodrich was to superintend a substantial overhaul and deepening in an effort to improve the supply.[54]

The work of constructing the well was completed on 28 January 1801.[55] Bentham intended the well to supply water to a grid of 8, 6 and 4in (203, 152 and 102mm) pipes laid round the dockyard. This scheme was estimated to cost £6,403 and was approved by the Navy Board in December 1801. By then Bentham had been sufficiently encouraged by the flow of water to suggest to Nepean that the water mains should be extended to the wharf edges to allow warships to replenish their supplies more easily. These pipes are shown as thin single lines on Fig 2.4. To provide a constant pressure in the mains, Bentham proposed a cistern capable of holding 200 tons (203 metric tons) of water should be sited on top of one of the engine houses. Such a cistern was probably not constructed until a year or two later, when the whole range of buildings here was remodelled and expanded.[56]

Although primarily intended to supply fresh water, part of the purpose of the well was to provide water for

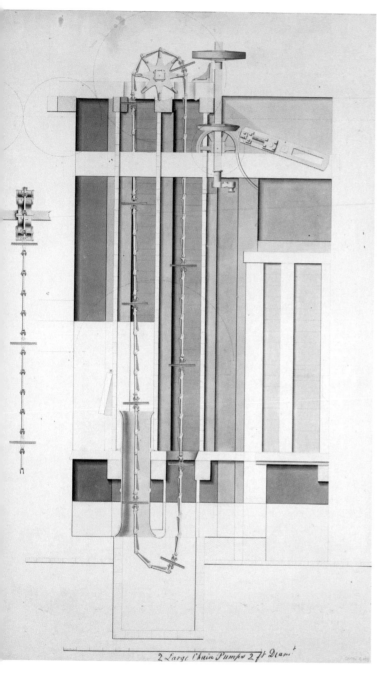

2 Large Chain Pumps 2 ft Diam.t

fire-fighting. For such circumstances, when the demand for water might be greater than the capacity of the well, Bentham designed a link to the main dock pumps that would allow them to feed salt water into the mains. Drawings for separate pumps for fresh and salt water were supplied to the dockyard officers in January 1802.[57] Much later, in August 1806, Goodrich saw 'the trial of the extinguishing engine . . . and the trial of the jet produced from the cisterns over the Woodmills from a fire cock near the jetty. It produced a jet as high as the two-storey building . . . The Jet was a large one from one of the largest branch pipes'.[58]

Despite all these activities, by the end of 1801 impressive evidence of the navy having entered the steam age was not immediately apparent to any observer in Portsmouth. The small and heterogeneous cluster of brick buildings, with its chimneys and engine and boiler houses of different sizes and designs, was crammed onto the site of the old horse pumps. In its centre was the vast stone-lined well shaft with its massive chain pumps for emptying the reservoir. Compared to the grand storehouses and workshops recently completed as part of the main dockyard modernisation programme, these buildings were small in scale and had few architectural pretensions. The Boulton and Watt engine house was the firm's standard economical design that appealed to frugal mine and mill owners. Probably many observers assumed that the completion of the installation of the second engine marked the end of this project (Fig 2.14). The more observant, though, must have wondered as to the purpose of the great series of brick vaults then being constructed within the reservoir itself.

Figure 2.12 (left) The cross-section of the chain pumps. This shows the horizontal drive to the deep freshwater well south-east of the building, and the reciprocating drive for the salt-water pump. (Science Museum/ Science and Society Picture Library, GC, C 101, No. 2)

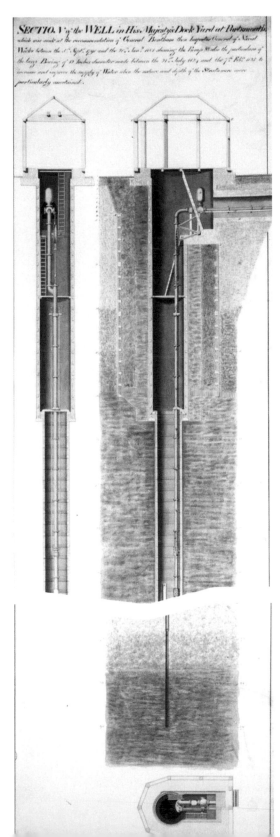

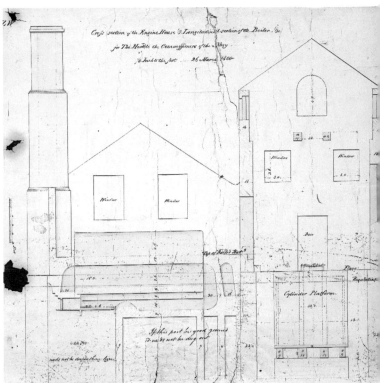

Figure 2.13 (left)
A section of the great freshwater well, showing the upper chamber, 25ft (7.6m) in diameter. This remarkable feat of excavation was finished on 28 January 1801 at a depth of 274ft (83.5m) from the surface. Its pump was powered by a drive from the Wood Mills some 400ft (120m) to the north-west. (Science Museum/Science and Society Picture Library)

Figure 2.14 (above)
A Boulton and Watt drawing showing the cross-section of the proposed 30hp beam engine and boiler house, dated 26 March 1800. This section is looking west. (The National Archives (PRO), ADM 140/504)

3 NEW SPACE AND
NEW OPPORTUNITIES

To Bentham, dock pumping must have been in many ways the least interesting part of his new enterprise. By 1800 the technology of steam pumping, if new to the navy, was well established in the outside world. If Bentham was to justify his new department, he had to do far more than simply import established technology to the royal dockyards: he had to demonstrate innovative manufacturing and material-processing that would have an immediate impact on warship construction and repair. Mechanise and modernise had to be his watchwords. But lack of space on this cramped Portsmouth site made this impracticable. The only possible solution lay in making use of the huge area occupied by the reservoir, estimated by Bentham at 35,000ft^2 (3,252m^2). As he noted in September 1799, 'the only part of this Excavation which is at all wanted or can be used for the purpose for which it was made is the very lowest part extending not more than 7 or 8 feet in height; the whole of the space above is worse than useless and may be considered as a gulph interrupting communication in the most central part of the yard'.[1] A few years before, the architect Samuel Wyatt had reached the same conclusion and had suggested the use of 'Messrs Bolton and Watt's fire engine' for dock pumping, sawing and various other purposes, and recommended that 'the present reservoir which is in bad repair, may be made into a tank by building pillars and arching it over by which means the large space of ground it occupies would become useful'.[2]

It is probable that Bentham was aware of Wyatt's scheme. In September 1799 he revived it but in a more elaborate form. Rather than the single tier of vaults of the original proposal, Bentham suggested two tiers. The lower tier would cover the sump, while the upper tier (Fig 3.1) could be used as lay-apart space for ships' stores that would otherwise have to be sold at the end of the war because of lack of storage space in the dockyard. Bentham also saw the upper tier having a use for storing flammable materials such as tar, pitch and rosin. Here it could be easily flooded in case of fire. He suggested this upper tier could be built for £16,000.[3] When consulted, however, the Portsmouth Dockyard officers, although welcoming the extra space to be gained at yard level by roofing the reservoir, queried the economic justification. The Navy Board itself felt that damp in the vaults would preclude their use for storage. Bentham dismissed this latter concern, adding that he would provide ducts from the upper tier of vaults to the engine house so that air would be sucked through to the boiler fires.[4] Time, however, was

to prove the Navy Board right in this instance. The real justification for vaulting the reservoir, as Bentham wrote in his September submission, was that the extra space gained at yard level would enable him to install his woodworking machinery: 'no other spot could be so well suited on account of its vicinity to the pumping apparatus, since by this means the same steam engine may be made to serve the double purpose of pumping the docks and working the machinery'. Bentham concluded this letter to the Admiralty by writing, 'I would further take the liberty of stating to their Lordships that the whole arrangement of my plan for erecting a system of machinery in this dockyard depends

Figure 3.1 Part of the upper tier of the vaults built over the reservoir. Circular openings allowed access to both levels. The sloping stone wall is part of the 1770s platform for the horse pumps. (EH, AA 042385)

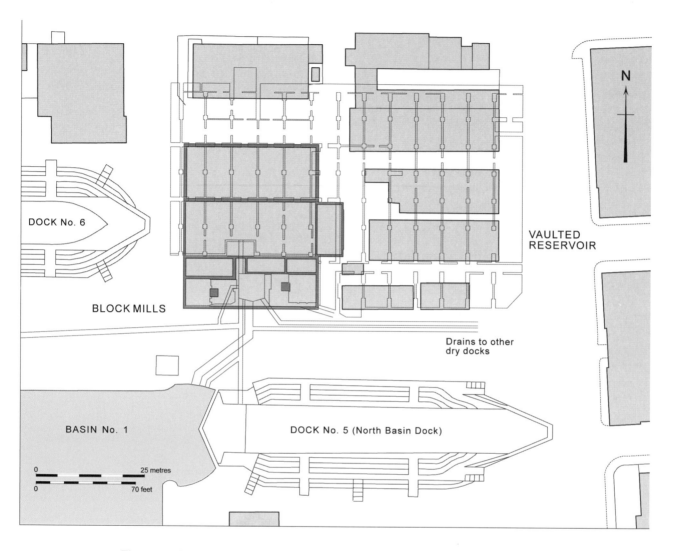

Figure 3.2 A modern plan showing (in red) the extent of the vaulted reservoir. (EH)

DOCK No. 6

VAULTED
RESERVOIR

BLOCK MILLS

Drains to other
dry docks

BASIN No. 1

DOCK No. 5 (North Basin Dock)

0   25 metres
0   70 feet

N

upon their decision respecting the expediency of covering over the reservoir'[5] (Fig 3.2).

In the spring of 1800 both the Admiralty and Navy Boards approved the scheme. Construction of the vaults was, perhaps surprisingly, not put out to contract but was undertaken by the dockyard labour force directed by the master shipwright, Henry Peake. He was working to plans apparently provided by Samuel Bunce, a member of Bentham's small staff and the navy's first salaried architect.[6] There are tantalisingly few references in the records to what must have been a very major civil engineering project, no doubt made more difficult by the need to

retain the reservoir in use. Annual estimates show that, in 1801, £10,000 was allocated for work on the vaults, and diminishing amounts appear every year until 1805.[7] Some form of coffer dam must have been used to allow construction of the foundations and piers of the lower vaults, perhaps similar to a temporary dam then being used during the enlargement of the adjacent Great Basin.[8] In August 1802 there was a setback caused by the collapse of seven masonry piers, blamed by Bentham in part on lack of supervision due to the illness of Henry Peake.[9]

By the spring of 1802 Bentham was already drawing up plans for his new Wood Mills. The Extra Estimates for that

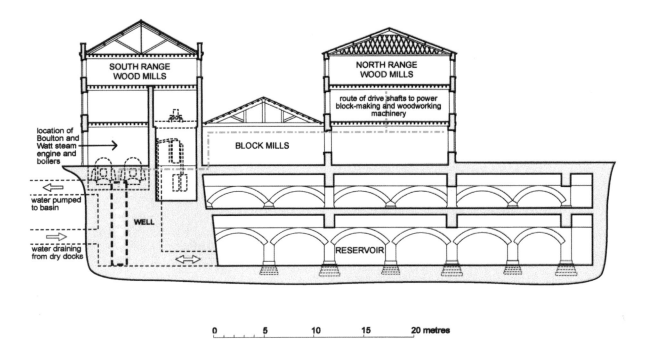

Figure 3.3 A section through the Wood Mills/Block Mills today that clearly shows the extent of the vaults beneath the building. The thick walls with offsets in the southern range of the Wood Mills (to the left) belong to the Boulton and Watt engine house. (EH)

Figure 3.4 Elevation of north wall of south range built over upper vaults of the reservoir and pump platform, looking south. The red shaded areas show the position of the engine houses. (EH)

year allocated £7,600 'to erect buildings over the reservoir for carrying on various works by machinery'.[10] In April, Bentham estimated these would cost £8,827, and by then he considered that the vaults were sufficiently advanced to allow construction to start.[11] The ensuing collapse of some of the piers in August had no effect on the new building, for, as Bentham reported to the Admiralty following his inspection of the damage, 'in consequence of my directions ... the foundation walls of the new building over the Reservoir have been proceeded with as fast as possible, and they are already brought up from the bottom, through the arches, so as to support the whole of the superstructure independently of them'[12] (Figs 3.3 and 3.4).

The new Wood Mills which the Admiralty authorised in April 1802 were designed as two parallel and matching three-storey, brick-built ranges, three bays wide, with a secure fenced area in between that was to be used to store timber. The existing engine and boiler houses were subsumed within the southern building, which, save for the two tall chimneys above its roof, gave no hint as to its purpose. The same reticence is apparent in the northern range. Ornament in both buildings is limited to stone cills, copings and string courses. Both in design and scale, the Wood Mills are highly conservative, looking back to the 18th-century dockyard workshops and storehouses rather than forward to the new steam age. They would, however, have met with the approval of an earlier Navy Board which had exhorted the dockyard officers to make their

new buildings 'plain, strong and convenient'.[13] Apart from their machinery, the buildings differed in one significant respect from contemporary and earlier dockyard buildings. Above their second floors each had water tanks nearly 100ft (30m) long, one 41ft (12.5m) wide, the other 38ft (11.6m) wide. These were to provide a head of water for Bentham's dockyard water main and for a fire-fighting system within the Wood Mills themselves. In 1808 Goodrich noted that each tank was generally filled to a depth of 18in (457mm), but 'might hold more if it were prudent'.[14] The buildings were almost certainly designed by the architect on Bentham's staff, Samuel Bunce, but he would have worked closely both with Bentham and with Simon Goodrich, Bentham's mechanical engineer. The drawings for the Wood Mills were certainly prepared in London and not by the dockyard officers, as would have been normal before the establishment of the inspector general's department.[15]

Construction of the Wood Mills occupied most of the short interlude of peace between the conclusion of the war with Revolutionary France and the outbreak of the Napoleonic Wars (Figs 3.5 and 3.6). The work was pressed ahead, as were other dockyard projects, for there was a widespread feeling that the Treaty of Amiens (1802) was unlikely to last. When Britain declared war on 17 May 1803, the two ranges of the Wood Mills were substantially complete, and some of Bentham's woodworking machinery was installed. Although none of it survives and no early floor plans of the buildings are known, references

Figure 3.5 Part of the upper tier of vaults beneath the Wood Mills, showing various stone-lined openings in the vaults. Some of these may be for machinery, but the one to the right may have been designed to suck air through the vaults to the steam-engine boiler houses. (EH, AA 042386)

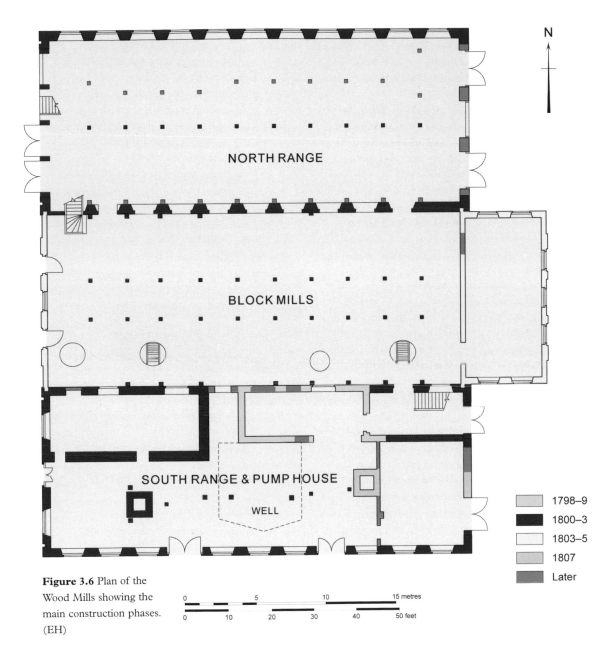

N

NORTH RANGE

BLOCK MILLS

SOUTH RANGE & PUMP HOUSE

WELL

	1798–9
	1800–3
	1803–5
	1807
	Later

Figure 3.6 Plan of the Wood Mills showing the main construction phases. (EH)

0   5   10   15 metres

0   10   20   30   40   50 feet

make it clear that this machinery was mostly located in the northern range. The ground floor of the southern range was largely taken up by steam engines, boilers and pumps . There is evidence that power was transmitted to the northern range by a drive shaft through the upper vaults of the reservoir.[16] There is also an 1815 reference suggesting that some power may have been transmitted by rope drive.[17] (See Appendix for a discussion of the drives of the building.)

In the letter of 22 April 1802 informing the Portsmouth officers that construction of the Wood Mills had been authorised, the Navy Board mentioned that 'a considerable part of the machinery ordered for your yard has long been ready for fixing up'.[18] This is one of the very few references in the official Navy Board records to some of the machinery of his own design that Bentham intended to install in the Wood Mills. Just over a year later, in June 1803, is a further tantalising reference when the Navy Board sends plans of 'three engines, forming a part of the machinery for working the wood', designed by Bentham. The Portsmouth officers are instructed to have yard workmen make the frames, a clear indication these were to be of timber.[19]

Bentham's early experience in the dockyards had shown him that the handling and preparation of timber in the royal dockyards was one of the most labour-intensive processes. The average oak tree that was felled for shipbuilding produced about one 'load' of timber, which was converted into approximately two-thirds of a ton of finished timber on a ship. The 2,162 tons (2,197 metric tons) of HMS *Victory* had required around 3,000 trees.[20] All this timber had to be prepared by hand, the initial sawing of the great tree trunks undertaken by teams of pit-sawyers. It was scarcely surprising that Bentham's energies were directed to seeing if mechanical means could be employed to increase productivity and efficiency. The new Wood Mills were to be his workshop and test-bed, if successful, progenitor of similar installations in the other major dockyards.

Although the fame of Brunel's block-making machinery was to eclipse Bentham's own inventions at Portsmouth, the latter are of considerable interest. His machinery was largely centred on methods of sawing timber. His saws divided into two main types: reciprocating saws and circular saws, with a third hybrid swing or pendulum saw. All of these had their advantages and limitations, and Goodrich's journals are full of references to these.

The development of circular saws was then very much in its infancy. Their advantage lay in their potential accuracy, speed and lack of vibration. However, their maximum size was comparatively small – limited by a combination of contemporary metal technology that restricted the size of the saw blade, and the need for a rigid frame. Bentham designed for Portsmouth a long-bed circular saw, with a saw 36in (9144mm) in diameter, and a number of smaller ones like modern bench saws for use by the joiners. The largest saw Goodrich mentions in the early years is a 21in (533mm) saw in use in 1804. This would indicate a maximum cutting depth of no more than about 9in (230mm). This tallies with a contemporary list of timbers to be cut by the circular saws at the Wood Mills. The largest timber mentioned is 8in² (5,161mm²).[21] However, progress with the development of circular saws was rapid. By late 1806 Brunel was experimenting at Portsmouth with a saw with a diameter of 6ft (1.8m) and wrote that 'I have one to hand of 9ft [2.74m] diameter'.[22] Initially, Brunel

had these very large circular saws constructed from six segmental shaped sections of blade, each secured to a central spindle by two small bolts and attached to each other by pairs of flat-headed screws. A note attached to a drawing of this arrangement stated that 'the plates cannot be fixed with too much nicety'.[23] It must have taken some courage to test the capabilities of these vast blades, as an alarming event on 29 November 1805 was to show. Goodrich noted:

As Mr Brunel was trying his large circular saw by accident, as it was in quick motion, it ran foul of a piece of timber on the drag and shattered 3 of the plates to pieces and bent the others. It was composed of 8 plates thus [a small sketch appears in the original] jointed by [sic] into each other by a V groove and edge – the noise occasioned by its breaking was like the report of a Gun. No other mischief was done.[24]

Brunel later complained to Maudslay about the quality of the timber baulks with which he had been supplied to test circular saws. Many had hidden nails or bits of gravel which blunted the teeth of the blades, so requiring frequent resharpening.[25]

Not until early 1807 did the more cautious Goodrich feel confident that it would be possible to obtain good-quality circular-saw blades that would not blunt themselves at high speed. This confidence was kindled by a visit to Maudslay's factory, where he saw a new iron furnace and a stamping press 'in which he stamps or cuts out the teeth of circular saws which he has undertaken to manufacture in a manner superior to the Common'. Much of this superiority lay in the subsequent heat-treatment processes that hardened and tempered the blades by a series of operations that heated them red-hot and dipped them in troughs of oil before hammering them and grinding them.[26]

In contrast to the comparatively small sizes of most of the early circular saws, reciprocating saws that mimicked the action of the pit-sawyers were being constructed with substantial blades. In 1804 Goodrich mentions blades more than 4ft (1.2m) long and with widths of 7in (178mm).[27] By mounting these parallel to each other in adjustable frames, substantial logs could be turned into a variety of different sizes of timber. Limitations were related to the strength and rigidity of the saw-frames and the speed of operation. The reciprocating motion, provided by a cranked drive, produced far more vibrations than was the case with a circular saw. Such vibrations largely governed the maximum

BLOCK MACHINERY at PORTSMOUTH.

Sawing Machine.

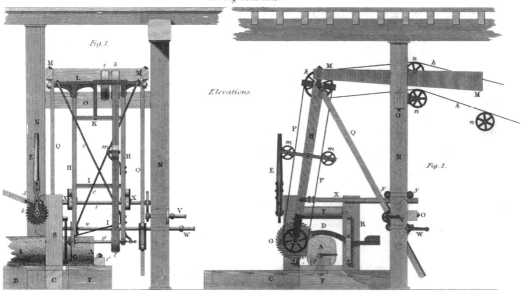

Elevations.

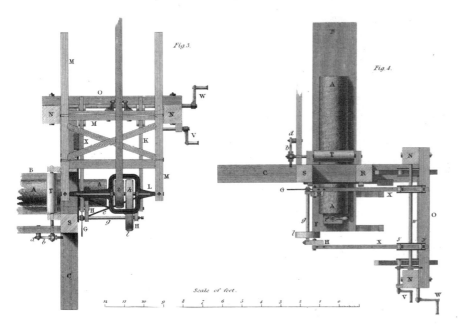

Scale of feet.

Published as the Act directs 1812 by Longman, Hurst, Rees, Orme, & Brown, Paternoster Row.

Engraved by Wilson Lowry.

Figure 3.7 Bentham's pendulum or swing saw. (Rees's *Cyclopaedia*, 1812)

speed at which the saws could be operated.

Bentham also constructed a horizontal reciprocating saw, for cuttting slices across a tree trunk. These slices were then cut up into pieces for making block shells. It mirrored the action of a carpenter using a hand saw, but cut on the back stroke. Brunel designed a smaller, more precise, saw for cutting sheave blanks.

In an attempt to combine the depth of cut attainable from a reciprocating saw with the speed and lack of vibration of a circular saw, Bentham designed an ingenious compromise called a swing or pendulum saw (Fig 3.7). Depending on the length required, the log was held firmly in a frame. A circular saw, mounted on an adjustable timber arm that could swing over the log, was then guided to make three cuts, one on each side of the log and one across the top. This method allowed the cutting of a log of greater diameter than would have been possible with a

fixed circular saw.[28] Its operation was similar to a modern radial arm saw, although this is less versatile in that it is able to make only horizontal cuts. In October 1806 Goodrich mentions that a swing saw was to replace 'Mr Brunel's large saw'. Concern about the fire risks here is evident in the next note: 'A 3inch iron pipe to be brought down from the cisterns over the Wood Mills . . . with two fire cocks at each floor, one with a hose constantly secured upon it.'[29]

On 3 October 1805 Marc Brunel was to list both circular saws and swing saws in the Wood Mills. His interest in these lay in using them for the initial timber preparation for his block-making machinery.[30] It is clear that he collaborated closely with Bentham and suggested a number of modifications.[31] Brunel also designed his own circular saws. In some exasperation, Goodrich records in June 1806: 'Brunel has also got another large Circular Saw

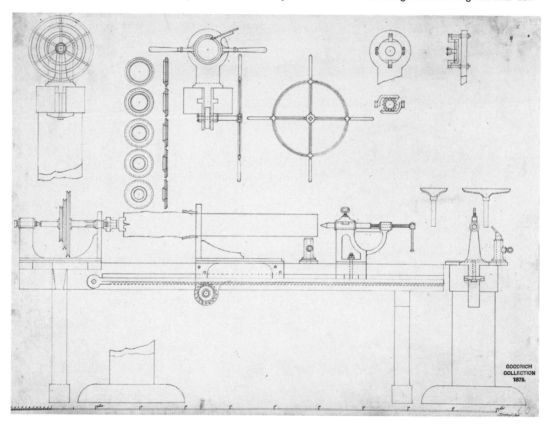

Figure 3.8 Contemporary drawing of a treenail lathe. In essence, this is a wood-turning lathe with an added slide, operated by a rack and pinion, moved by turning the capstan wheel. The cutter blade was fixed in the holder on the upright part of the slide. A collet centred the turned wood as it passed through the body of the slide. (Science Museum/Science and Society Picture Library, GC, C 60)

sent down to be tried this the third'.[32] This perhaps suggests that there were problems, but the comparative absence of reference to saws in the Goodrich papers after around 1809 may indicate that by then these had been overcome.

To help manoeuvre the largest timber in the sawmilling area and to feed them into the saws, Bentham installed at least one small capstan on the ground floor of the Wood Mills. This is described as being 1ft (305mm) in diameter 'in the smallest part'. Its drive was to be so arranged 'as to cause the feed to advance one foot in one second'.[33] If this is an accurate record of the feed rate it demonstrates clearly the advantages of power sawing over pit-sawing.

Although Bentham's interests in wood machinery are known to have extended beyond saws, an 1818 list of machines in the Wood Mills mentions only the block-making machinery and the following saws: '1 cross-cut saw, 1 Swing-saw, 1 Up and Down saw, 3 Circular saws, 2 Circular saw Machines for converting Lignum Vitae, 1 horizontal ditto [sic]'.[34]

This may, however, be an incomplete list. In March 1806 a treenail lathe had been sent to Portsmouth. Later, Goodrich noted that it was in the Wood Mills and 'is worked by the steam engine and all the treenails for Portsmouth Yard are I believe made by it'.[35] Treenails were the long timber pegs used to fasten a warship's hull timbers together. These were produced in lengths that varied from 12 to 36in (305 to 915mm). In 1814 Goodrich noted that one man could produce between 200 and 250 of the longest treenails in a day.[36] Essentially, a treenail machine operated like a hybrid lathe and giant pencil sharpener, a cutter – like a very large pencil sharpener – rounding the timber, which was fixed in a horizontal position (Fig 3.8). The treenail machine that is in the Block Mills today may be this 1806 machine (Fig 3.9). Goodrich ascribes the introduction of these machines to Bentham, but, surprisingly, noted that as late as 1814 treenails were still being produced manually at Portsmouth by one man and a boy using spokeshaves. It was apparently only then that the mechanical production of treenails finally replaced the skilled craftsman.[37]

Figure 3.9 The treenail machine in the Block Mills. This may be the one referred to in 1806. A partly formed treenail can be seen passing through the cutter and collet. Different sized collets could be substituted, depending on the required diameters of the treenails. (EH, AA 042412)

4 MARC BRUNEL AND THE MANUFACTURE OF SHIPS' BLOCKS

By a strange coincidence, on 14 April 1802, the same day that the Portsmouth officers were authorised to begin construction of the Wood Mills on top of the reservoir, Bentham was writing to the Admiralty enthusiastically endorsing a revolutionary scheme for manufacturing ships' blocks. Its subsequent implementation in Portsmouth Dockyard firmly placed the Royal Navy at the forefront of technical progress. The partial transformation of the Wood Mills into the Block Mills was to give the Royal Navy the first full-scale factory in the world to use machine tools for mass production.

Ships' blocks – pulley blocks – were then used in huge quantities by the Royal Navy. A 74-gun warship had no fewer than 922 for her standing and running rigging and about 450 for working the guns; a first-rate such as HMS *Victory* required around 1700. By the opening years of the 19th century the Royal Navy's annual requirement for blocks was around 100,000. Although nearly every royal dockyard employed a few block-makers, these men spent most of their time repairing and overhauling blocks from warships undergoing refit or from warships being brought out of ordinary. It is doubtful if any dockyard manufactured more than a few blocks from new. Instead, the Royal Navy purchased its requirements from outside suppliers. By the end of the 18th century the supply of blocks was monopolised by two firms, Bartholomew Dunsterville at Plymouth and Taylor at Southampton.

Blocks were made up of three main components: a sheave or pulley, turning on a pin set within a shell or casing (Fig 4.1). The shell itself, made of elm wood, was scored on its external surface to hold a rope strap. The sheave was lignum vitae with a bell-metal bearing or coak set in its centre. The term bell metal appears in the contemporary literature, and has been used in this text, but the actual metal mixture cited by Goodrich was closer to gun metal (*see* Chapter 6, note 8). The pin was iron, or hardwood if intended for use in powder magazines. Blocks were some of the very few manufactured items needed in standard sizes and in very large quantities by the fleet. As such, they were ideally suited to mass-production methods. Both of the principal suppliers of blocks to the navy made limited use of machinery. At Southampton, Samuel Taylor (1734–1803) used horse-driven machinery (Fig 4.2),

Figure 4.1 A double block in the rigging of HMS Victory. (EH, AA049702)

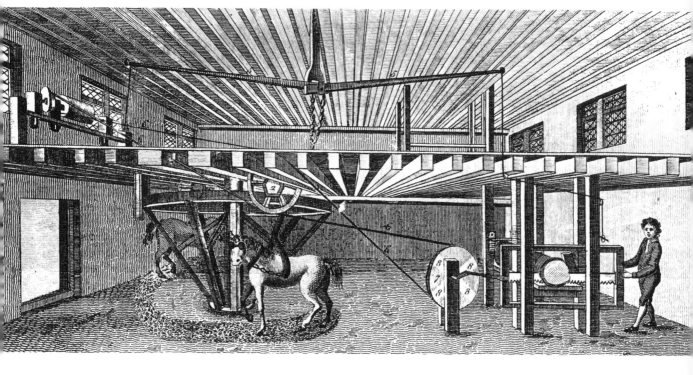

Figure 4.2 A horse-powered saw in operation at Taylor's block-making factory. This was the only part of the block-making process to be mechanised before the invention of Brunel's machinery. Machinery was also used to a limited extent at Bartholomew Dunsterville's block mills at Plymouth and at Roper's manufactory at Houndsditch. (From Steel, D, *The Elements and Practise of Rigging and Seamanship*, London, 1794; reproduced in Gilbert 1965, 3, Fig 2, Science Museum/Science and Society Picture Library)

principally for sawing, and is credited as one of the inventors of the circular saw. Dunsterville at Plymouth likewise made extensive use of saws of various types, as well as lathes for turning the sheaves and boring machines for the sheaves and coaks.[1] That, however, was the limit; manufacturing of blocks, especially the shells, still remained largely a craft industry, heavily dependent on the skills of the workforce.

In early 1799 the young French emigré Marc Brunel left New York, where he had been chief engineer, to try for his fortune in Britain (Fig 4.3). In America his inventive mind had become absorbed in designing block-making machinery, but the mass market for such blocks potentially was far greater in Britain, with its vastly larger mercantile and naval fleets. On arrival in London, he renewed his acquaintance with Sophie Kingdom, whom he had last seen in France, and in November 1799 they were married. Earlier that year, in his first stroke of good fortune, a fellow emigré, named

De Bacquancourt, knowing Brunel's engineering interests, introduced him to Henry Maudslay (Fig 4.4), who had a small engineering workshop in Wells Street, north of Oxford Street. Henry Maudslay was probably the finest mechanical engineer in Britain at that time. Brunel was to commission him to produce scale models of his proposed machinery (see figs 6.12 and 6.14), reasoning correctly that if he was to interest people, models would be far more persuasive than engineering drawings. The superbly engineered and detailed working metal models that Maudslay ultimately produced can now be seen in the National Maritime Museum in Greenwich. Most of 1800 was spent by Brunel working on his block-making design drawings and commissioning models from Maudslay. By early February 1801 Brunel felt sufficiently confident of his inventions to take out a patent (No. 2478). The patent drawings show that the machines bore little resemblance to the machines as built for Portsmouth. They were all

Figure 4.3 Marc Brunel, a portrait painted *c*1812. To his left is a mortising machine. (© National Portrait Gallery, London, 978)

Figure 4.4 Henry Maudslay. His skills as a manufacturer of machine tools were crucial to Brunel's success. (© National Portrait Gallery, London, D1378)

wood-framed, and very crude. There is some confusion about the number of models Maudslay initially made: indeed in a letter dated 20 August 1801 Brunel wrote to the Admiralty asking for money to make models of a further seven machines to complete the set.[2] According to Farey, writing in Rees's *Cyclopaedia* in 1812, there was in addition a model steam engine supplied to drive the models when they were demonstrated. This is now lost.

In his quest to interest others in his proposed block-making machines, Brunel's second stroke of good fortune was his marriage. Sophie's brother John was chief clerk in the Secretary's Office in the Navy Board and it was John who originally approached the Taylors on Marc's behalf. In March 1801 Samuel Taylor rejected the suggestions that he might use Brunel's new machines, confident in the superiority of his own production methods. It was a mistake he was to regret.[3]

It seems likely that Brunel spent much of the remainder of the year working with Maudslay on the production not just of further models, but also of one full-size machine.[4]

Early in 1802, Brunel approached Bentham with his ideas. Bentham, excited by what he learnt when he visited Brunel, recommended that he approach the Board of Admiralty.[5] In the spring of 1802, Brunel secured an audience with the board, taking at least one model and possibly a full-size machine with him, and demonstrating them to the assembled commissioners. It is not certain whether Bentham attended this meeting, but his earlier visit to Brunel's house had enabled him to appreciate the significance of the machinery, and he would no doubt have advised the board beforehand. Bentham had to leave for Plymouth shortly afterwards. From there, he wrote to Evan Nepean with his views on the Brunel proposals:

on examination of the machinery invented by Mr Brunel, and exemplified not only by the small model which he exhibited to their Lordships, but also by a larger apparatus of a similar construction, and capable of making blocks for real use under the size of nine inches, I am convinced that his invention is well suited to the

51

purpose of manufacturing Blocks of all sizes with a degree of accuracy, uniformity and cheapness beyond what can be expected from the modes hitherto in use. . . . if a set of engines of different sizes, suitable to the manufacture of the different sizes of Blocks used in the Navy, were to be erected so as to form part of the system of machinery to be worked by the steam engines . . . already provided in Portsmouth Yard, I have no doubt but that the saving that would arise by the manufacture of blocks by these means would be as great as Mr Brunel has stated it to be.

I would therefore propose that Mr Brunel should be directed to concert with the Mechanist [Simon Goodrich] in my office respecting the best mode of fixing up the different Engines and Apparatus which may appear requisite for the manufacture of the different sorts and sizes of blocks, so that this Apparatus should combine with other Machinery already provided, or which it may seem advisable to erect in that Dock Yard; and that Mr Brunel may be likewise directed to give into my office drawings and estimates of the expense of the whole of the machinery which may appear to him necessary for this purpose. I should then be enabled to submit to their Lordships my further opinion respecting what had best be done for the introduction of this mode of making Blocks for the general service of the Dock Yards.

This was an enthusiastic letter. It was a generous one too, for block-making machinery also interested Bentham, who had written at the start of this letter, 'the making of blocks was one of the purposes for which it was intended to employ a part of the force of the steam engine erected in Portsmouth Dockyard'.[6] Presumably, Bentham had hoped to design such machines himself.

In his journal, Brunel wrote of the meeting that his proposals 'gave such satisfaction that my proposition of making a blockmill was adopted. Accordingly General Bentham took me to Portsmouth. Having had occasion then of seeing what had already been done of the steam engine and buildings, I made my disposition accordingly. But a most difficult task was to find some person fit for the execution of so extensive and so complicated an apparatus.[7] Finding skilled workmen was to be a recurring problem. For the next few years, starting in the early summer of 1802, there was to be a period of constant and close collaboration, although not always without its share of tensions, between Bentham, Brunel, Goodrich and Maudslay.

Although Brunel's proposals may have been endorsed by the Admiralty in the spring, it was not until early August that the dockyard officers at Portsmouth were instructed to proceed with the necessary building works that would allow the block-making machinery to be installed 'with as little delay as possible'.[8] To meet naval requirements and to cater for the variety of sizes of blocks, three different sized sets of machines were needed. The first, for blocks from 7 to 10in (178 to 254mm) long, were ordered in 1802 and were to be delivered in 1803. They were to be followed in 1804 by the machines for the smallest sizes of blocks, from 4 to 7in (102 to 178mm). Finally, for delivery in 1805, came the largest set of machines for blocks from 10 to 18in (254 to 457mm) long. In all, Maudslay was to manufacture some 45 machines for this series of contracts.[9]

The success of the block-making machines hinged in very large part on the quality of their materials and construction. By awarding Maudslay the contract for manufacturing the machinery, the Admiralty had secured the services of probably the best engineering workshop in the country. The quality of Maudslay's workmanship astonishes even today. A writer in 1824 stated that 'there is but another workman, perhaps, in the United Kingdom, who could have finished the engines in a manner so worthy of the invention'.[10] Many of these machines were to remain in production for over 150 years, finally being retired because of the lack of demand for blocks in the mid-20th-century navy, rather than from any faults or wear in the machinery itself. These machines and their operation will be discussed in Chapter 6.

Although not stated anywhere, one reason for the Portsmouth officers not receiving any instructions for further building works at the Wood Mills until August 1802 must have lain in the sheer novelty of the scheme. Brunel had convinced Bentham and the Admiralty of the benefits of the proposals, but the actual details all had to be worked out between Brunel and Bentham's staff. The idea of mass production using machine tools driven by a steam engine was wholly new. Calculations had to be made of the total number of machines, in the sets of various sizes, required to make the Royal Navy independent of outside contractors. Further calculations had to be made to ensure that particular types of machines were ordered in appropriate numbers to avoid production delays. Brunel's careful preparatory work over the previous few years must have provided answers to many of these questions, but much thought would have been given that summer to how these machines were to

Figure 4.5 The two three-storey ranges of Bentham's Wood Mills, showing the single-storey infill range added in 1802 to help house most of the new block-making machinery. (EH, AA 042378)

be located in Bentham's new Wood Mills. These were being constructed for other woodworking machinery of Bentham's own design; he no doubt was concerned about the total space available. When selecting locations for the machinery, consideration had to be given to how to link them to the various overhead and underground drive shafts from the steam plant. Thought also had to be given to the disposition of the various machines relative to each other – the phrase 'production line' had yet to be invented – but some sort of order of manufacturing had to be worked out so the process did not lead to confusion and unnecessary handling. Logically,

manufacturing had to start with the raw materials and end with the finished blocks. At best, this part of the operation had to have an empirical element, and there is some evidence for continuing modifications to the locations of individual machines in the early years of the manufacturing operation.

By August 1802, when the Portsmouth officers received their orders for further building work at the Wood Mills, Bentham's department had taken the decision to add a new single-storey building that would infill the storage yard between the two ranges of the Wood Mills (Fig 4.5). This would contain many, but not all, of the block

Figure 4.6 The interior of the central range looking west, *c*1900. At this date the central range is still predominantly given to the manufacture of the shells of the blocks. The row of machines on the left is arranged in production sequence: the boring machine has a pile of solid blocks of wood in front of it; beyond are mortising, cornering and shaping machines. The steam engines are in the south range beyond the wall on the left. (Portsmouth City Museums and Record Service)

machines. The rest would be housed in the north range. Bentham himself was in the dockyard that August, looking at further strengthening of the piers of the reservoir, possibly in connection with this additional structure, and undoubtedly took a lead with the dockyard officers in hastening work on the new building.[11] For its north and south sides, it made use of the existing walls of the Wood Mills, but its east and west elevations were given simple brick pediments with stone detailing. In itself, this use of pediments in contrast to the unrelieved severity of the

Wood Mills strongly suggests that Bentham was keen to emphasise the importance of the revolutionary process that the new building would contain. This point is made again inside, where the interior is notable for the turned wooden Tuscan columns that support the roof trusses (Figs 4.6 and 4.7). These columns have their bases set high perhaps so that they would not be obscured by machinery. These turned columns have no parallel in any other dockyard building of the period, and it is tempting to speculate that they may have been produced on some

Figure 4.7 The interior of the central range in 2003 looking east. This clearly shows the handsome turned wooden columns and the overhead line shafting. The latter probably dates mainly from the middle years of the 19th century, but its location and principle follow closely on the system devised by Bentham, Brunel and Goodrich by 1805. the south range and its engine houses are on the right. (EH, AA 042405)

of Bentham's new woodworking machinery. Certainly they also represent Bentham's awareness that what he was creating here would be a showpiece. This care extended ultimately to the disposition of the Brunel machinery itself, for Bentham was to write:

> I had considered it highly conducive to the hastening of the introduction of a general system of machinery, that public opinion should be obtained in its favour, and that this was likely to be more effected by a display of well arranged machines . . . I determined . . . the machines

which it might be expedient to employ exclusively for blockmaking admitted of a pleasing arrangement to point of appearance as well as use.[12]

Construction of this new central range cannot have taken long and it must have been complete before the arrival of the first Brunel machinery in 1803. Two further small additions were made before the complex achieved the form it retains to the present. By the middle of 1803 Brunel was asking Bentham for a resident engineer to maintain the new machinery. He would require a workshop 'which [if possible] should be on the same floor where the machines are fixed'. This should contain a forge and bellows, an anvil, vices, two hammers, a good foot lathe with drills and chucks, a large number of files, saws, dividers, compasses and a brace, as well as a supply of bars of blister steel.[13] This workshop was added to the eastern end of the central range and is notable for the generously sized eastern window, set partly into the pediment. A year later, the practical difficulties of access between the upper floors of the main north and south ranges (Fig 4.8) was addressed by Bunce's successor as architect, Edward Holl, who sent a sketch drawing to

Figure 4.8 One of the two original stairs in the building. These must have been the only route for timber products manufactured on the first floor to reach the main assembly area on the ground floor. This stair is at the western end of the south range (EH, AA 042429)

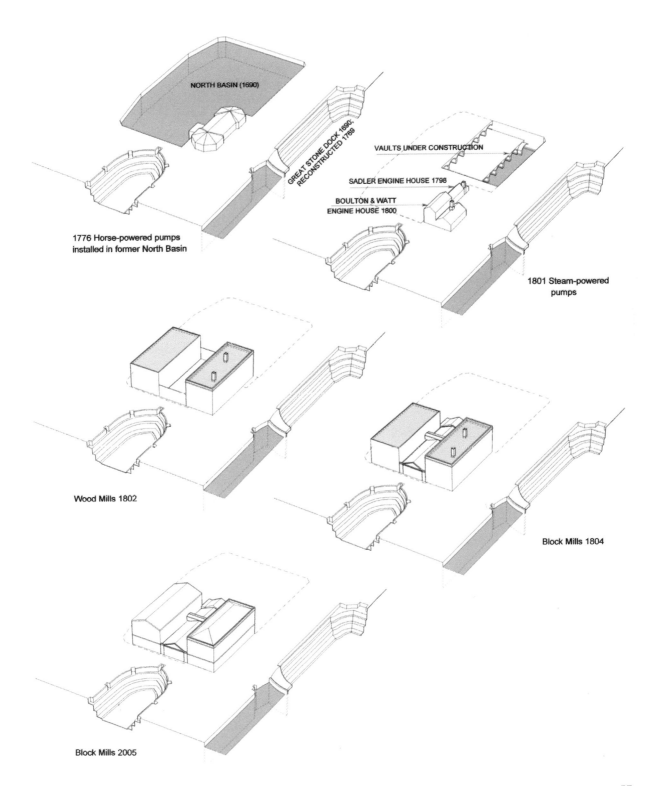

NORTH BASIN (1690)

1776 Horse-powered pumps installed in former North Basin

GREAT STONE DOCK 1690, RECONSTRUCTED 1769

VAULTS UNDER CONSTRUCTION

SADLER ENGINE HOUSE 1798

BOULTON & WATT ENGINE HOUSE 1800

1801 Steam-powered pumps

Wood Mills 1802

Block Mills 1804

Block Mills 2005

Figure 4.9 A schematic view of the development of the Block Mills site from 1776. (EH)

Goodrich at Portsmouth showing a passage. Although the sketch is not known to survive, this almost certainly relates to the weatherboarded passage that links the first floors, crossing partly through the roof space of the central range, incidentally giving users a fine bird's-eye view of the main floor below (Fig 4.9).[14]

Bentham's Wood Mills and these various additions all still stand. Within the south range are the remains of the earlier engine houses, the boiler houses and the great pump shaft. The building sequences are all clearly visible. There was to be a later addition of a single-storey range in the 1830s along the north side of the north range to house vertical

Figure 4.10 Looking towards the western end of the roof space above the south range. On the left is the capped-off chimney from the Boulton and Watt boiler house. The wooden floor may have once supported the large water tank known to have been installed at this level. In all probability the tank was formed of timber and lined with lead. It was probably dismantled in the 1840s, following the construction of the existing cast-iron water tank near Long Row, and was replaced by the existing roof. (EH, AA 042426)

Figure 4.11 Part of the second floor of the south range. The interior construction, with its use of massive timbers, is very typical of naval storehouses and workshops of the latter part of the 18th century. (EH, AA 042422)

saw-frames, but this was subsequently demolished. At the beginning of the 20th century, steam power was replaced by electricity, and the two boiler chimneys were reduced below roof level and capped (Fig 4.10). Possibly as a result of damage in the Second World War, the northern range had its parapets removed and was re-roofed using a lattice-truss system. Internally, there have been minor alterations to the fabric over the years as machinery and drive systems have been added, modified, replaced and repositioned (Fig 4.11). Here again, fixing marks on walls, floors and roof timbers provide clues.

Today, Bentham's Wood Mills and the central block-making range look much as they did when newly completed and visited by Nelson in September 1805. The only significant external differences are the additions of fire escapes, the absence of the boiler chimneys, and the later reforming of the roof. Below, the reservoir conversion of the 1770s is intact, although used less frequently; the pumps are now electric, but remains of the earlier machinery are still extant (Fig 4.12). If the buildings themselves are now silent, water can still sometimes be heard flowing underneath through the great vaulted chambers.

Bentham's wish for public appreciation for his new manufactory was to be answered, although not in a way that he may have intended. Within a few years of installation, Brunel's machinery was giving its name to the whole group of buildings. First in popular references, then increasingly in official records, Wood Mills as a term largely vanishes and is replaced by Block Mills.

Figure 4.12 The penstock controlling the main culvert from the dry docks into the reservoir. This view is looking north towards the central range. The wall on the left is the east wall of the 1800 Boulton and Watt engine house; that on the right is the west wall of the Sadler engine house. (EH, AA 042403)

5 THE CONSTRUCTION OF THE BLOCK MILLS, 1802–1807

When Bentham wrote to Evan Nepean in April 1802 endorsing Brunel's proposals for his new block-making machinery, he recommended that the latter liaise closely with his mechanist or engineer, Simon Goodrich.[1] Goodrich was then aged 29 and had worked for Bentham since December 1796, when he had been appointed as draughtsman to the mechanist. The first mechanist was Samuel Rehe, of Shoe Lane, Fleet Street, who had been a pupil of the scientific instrument maker Jesse Ramsden.[2] As well as his work on scientific instruments – he was especially skilled at the graduation of scales – he is known to have developed a machine for milling the teeth of gear wheels, and was the pioneer of inserted-teeth milling cutters.[3] One of Rehe's pupils was the Swiss J C Fischer,[4] who worked for him for a short while in 1794, when on his travels through industrial England. While there Fischer made parts for textile spinning machinery, such as roller spindles.[5] Rehe had the reputation of being a good mechanic and had initially supplied Bentham with materials and parts when he was developing his machines before he was appointed inspector general. Rehe was responsible for the erection of the Sadler engine, and a large lifting pump capable of raising 7 tons of salt water per minute (see Fig 2.10). He built the first experimental 2ft (610mm) diameter chain pump, and made a model materials-testing machine; he helped Bentham with technical advice.[6] Towards the middle of 1799 Rehe became ill and Goodrich, who had been appointed a draftsman to the mechanist by Bentham in December 1796, deputised for him. On the death of Rehe in October 1799, Goodrich was appointed in his place.[7]

On his appointment, Goodrich was given an annual salary of £400.[8] We know little of his early life, other than he was born in 1773 in Suffolk, apparently near Bury St Edmunds; he came from a large family and one of his brothers was miller at the Victualling Board's flour mill at Deptford.[9] How he came to the attention of Bentham is not known. It is possible that Bentham made it a condition of his appointment as mechanist that he made study tours to further his knowledge. The diary of perhaps his first tour, made in November/December 1799, is in the Goodrich Collection, and this shows he was a well-educated and highly literate man. There is much information about the power transmission in the Strutts' textile mills around Derby and other mills in Manchester, as well as about early machine tools. He commented on the use of lightweight cast-iron shafts and pulleys. In 1802 he entered the competition to redesign the Albion Mills,

London, which had burnt down in 1791; although he did not win the competition, his efforts were awarded a prize of 25 guineas. Clearly the experience and knowledge he had gained on his travels stood him in good stead later, when he took on the design of the power transmission at the Block Mills.[10]

Goodrich's career with the navy was to extend over some 35 years, much of it initially spent at Portsmouth looking after the Block Mills and the Metal Mills.[11] But his interests continued to range beyond the dockyard boundaries and he never seems to have lost his thirst for knowledge. He was keen to keep abreast with developments in industry throughout the British Isles, and he was well known to the country's leading scientists and engineers. In him Bentham had a capable and industrious assistant, moreover one who was held in considerable respect by his peers. His increasing mechanical and engineering knowledge made him the ideal person to collaborate with Brunel. Over the next few years, the establishment and operation of the Block Mills were to absorb a great deal of Goodrich's time.

In a report in 1806 to the Board of Revision, Goodrich gave a very full account of his duties. These show that he was in charge of all the works connected with the design and construction of the Boulton and Watt engine, the chain pumps, drains, penstocks and the dockyard piped water supply, including a separate supply for Haslar Hospital. He was also responsible for designing and preparing the drawings for the power transmission in the Wood Mills and 'concerting with the inventor of the machines for making Blocks, for their introduction and generally for the whole of the arrangements relative to the erection of these machines at Portsmouth Yard'. In addition, he worked closely with Bentham, providing the drawings and organising the erection of the various saws and other machinery. Away from Portsmouth, his mechanical skills took him to Plymouth, Deptford, Woolwich and the victualling yard at Dover. On top of all that, he had to check all the incoming bills to Bentham's office and deputise for the latter in his absences.[12]

In the course of 1800, as the machinery started to arrive at Portsmouth, Brunel and Goodrich, with Bentham's agreement, gradually built up a small team to help install, run and maintain it. As neither the Royal Navy nor the royal dockyards had hitherto required engineers, neither had a pool of trained talent from which to draw. Instead, likely people were selected on the basis of personal observation and word-of-mouth recommendations. Such was James Burr, one of Bentham's draughtsmen. He was, according to Brunel, who wrote to Bentham seeking his services for the project, 'well qualified for this duty, both on account of his knowledge of dockyard business, and on account of his being already so well practised in working wood by your machinery of various kinds'.[13] James Burr had been in the navy, and was then employed by Bentham to help make the pioneering machinery at his brother's house before he was appointed inspector general. In May 1796 Bentham wrote to the Navy Board requesting that he be appointed draughtsman to his department. Burr was later appointed master of the Wood Mills.[14]

William Barlow had been an employee of Maudslay and had worked erecting the Block Mills machinery. He was recommended by the master shipwright when the latter heard that Brunel was looking for someone to maintain the machinery. William Barlow was also considered by Bentham to be 'a workman of superior dexterity and experience'.[15] John Lloyd was a London millwright, of Chapel Street, Westminster, who had been employed by Bentham on the machinery at his brother's house. Lloyd always worked as a contractor for the Admiralty, and was never formally on Bentham's staff. In July 1796 he made the mortar mills for Portsmouth Dockyard, and in 1798 he helped construct Sadler's steam engine. In 1805 Bentham credited him with erecting most of the machinery at Portsmouth.[16] Burr, Lloyd and Barlow all seem to have joined the small team in the summer of 1803.

Another person to appear briefly at this point is Joshua Field. He was born at Hackney in 1786, and on completing his education in 1803, he started an engineering pupilage as a draughtsman in the inspector general's office under Goodrich. In 1804 he was transferred by the Admiralty to assist Maudslay in his workshops in the preparation of the detailed drawings for some of the block machines. He remained with Maudslay and in 1810 moved with him to his new workshops at Lambeth. In 1812 he became a partner, and in 1822 the firm's name was changed to Maudslay, Son and Field.[17]

In many ways, the most interesting member of the inspector general's staff was James Sadler, who was appointed as chemist in 1796 (Fig 5.1). He made his name as a balloonist, but also worked in the chemical laboratory at Oxford University, where he was closely associated with Thomas Beddoes. Beddoes and William Reynolds, a partner at Coalbrookdale, encouraged Sadler in the development of his steam engine. Several Sadler engines were erected there and also in London between 1792 and 1799. He was

Figure 5.1 James Sadler in 1820, some eleven years after he had left Bentham's staff. By an unknown artist. (© National Portrait Gallery, London, 4955)

threatened by Boulton and Watt for infringing their patent, but they did not proceed to court action. Sadler took out a patent for a kind of reaction wheel – a Barker's mill[18] – and according to Farey he took out another patent in 1798 for a twin cylinder engine, one atmospheric and the other on the Cartwright principle.[19]

In 1795 Sadler was appointed barracks master at Portsmouth, and in the following year was engaged by Bentham. From 1796 he was involved in experiments in naval ordnance, particular for the armaments Bentham introduced on his experimental vessels. In later years in his role as chemist, Sadler was involved in investigating copper sheathing, sea-water distillation, timber seasoning, combustion of gunpowder, air pumps and signal lights. According to Torrens his relationship with Bentham was not happy, but he continued in post until 1809, when he was dismissed.[20]

The rest of the staff included John and Henry Peake, who came from a long established shipbuilding family.

Henry Peake was appointed a surveyor to the navy in 1806. John Peake returned to the Admiralty around December 1808 with the title of extra assistant civil architect and engineer. This post was abolished in 1812.[21]

Although we know the names of many of the supervisory staff, the first actual machine operators remain anonymous. One of the great attractions of Brunel's machines for the Admiralty was the promised cost-savings, achieved in part by the use of unskilled labour. This too had appealed to Bentham, who 'as he had done in Russia, consciously "built skill into" his machines so as to make them suitable for fast precise operation by Russian peasants . . . or any other unskilled operators'.[22] Such an approach not only made practical sense when skilled operatives were few, but it no doubt also owed something to his brother Jeremy's utilitarian philosophy. A few years later, when teething problems had been largely overcome, 10 workmen using the block-making machines were said to have equalled the work of 110 skilled craftsmen.[23]

From the correspondence and journals of Bentham, Brunel and Goodrich it is possible to follow in some detail the trials, tribulations and ultimate success of this pioneering project. As has already been mentioned, Brunel had designed three different sized sets of his machines which between them could manufacture the full range of block sizes required by the fleet.

On August 2 1802 the Admiralty ordered the Navy Board to proceed with the necessary works to allow Brunel's block-making machinery to be put into production.[24] At that stage, the buildings were still under construction and were not to be completed until 1803. In October 1802 the architect Samuel Bunce died.[25] Over the next few months, it seems probable that Bentham himself may well have had to supervise some of their design and construction, for by December he was writing to Nepean saying that he could not carry the architectural load of the office and asking that Edward Holl be appointed to supervise works in the London area.[26]

Completing the actual buildings was the easiest part of the project. Brunel had designed his new machinery to be of all-metal construction to ensure that it would be robust and durable, and would function with a very high degree of reliability and accuracy. At that time, it was normal for metal to be used for the moving parts of machinery, but machine frames were invariably made of wood. The comparatively sophisticated work that the individual machines were required to undertake also demanded a high degree of manufacturing skill on the part of the

machine-maker. At this stage of the Industrial Revolution in Georgian England, such skills were rare. Already by September 1802, Brunel was writing to the Navy Board about 'The difficulty I have met in procuring a sufficient number of able workmen to execute the block machinery'. To Bentham he wrote, 'In order to execute with expedition the apparatus I am ordered to erect, I shall be under the necessity of dividing the several parts composing it to various persons. If you have any particularly able person whom I can trust with some part of the machinery, I shall be much obliged of you to inform me of it'. This correspondence suggests that at this stage Brunel may have been uncertain if Maudslay had the capacity to manufacture all the machines in time. If so, it was a short-lived uncertainty. He added 'I take the liberty of pointing out Mr Maudslay as a man whose abilities can be relied upon for the execution of such part of the machinery that will require the greatest exactness'.[27]

Bentham's own long experience, combined with his earlier inspection of Maudslay's models of the block-making machinery, no doubt enabled him to back Brunel's judgement on this last point. Although machined parts for the actual blocks themselves were for a time to be procured from outside manufacturers, there is no indication that, from this point on, anyone other than Maudslay was considered as a possible manufacturer of the block-making machinery itself. His choice was no doubt made easier by the circumstances of Brunel's contract with the Admiralty. Payment for the first set of machines was made through Brunel, with moneys advanced by Bentham from his departmental budget. The second and third sets were paid for directly by the Navy Board, but by the time these were ordered, the quality of Maudslay's work and the capacity of his workshop were self-evident.[28]

In March 1803 Maudslay was able to dispatch the first set of machines to Portsmouth.[29] Installation at Portsmouth was Brunel's responsibility, assisted by Goodrich, Barlow and Burr. Bentham himself was frequently in the dockyard that year. It was not just the Block Mills that demanded his attention. Nearby, work was under way on the navy's first metal mills, built and equipped to his designs. These were to smelt iron and copper and to roll the latter for sheathing the hulls of the warships. In September 1803 Bentham was able to report that the copper furnace had successfully smelted its first 4 ton load.[30] In due course, part of the Metal Mills' output would be used for producing the metal coaks and pins needed by the Block Mills.

Towards the end of May 1803, Brunel was able to write to Nepean and tell him that the machinery for the 7 to 10in (178 to 254mm) blocks was now complete. He also enclosed a list of further machines for making 'blocks, dead-eyes, trucks and other block-makers wares . . . of the several sizes and dimensions used in His Majesty's Navy':

3 Engines for boring holes in the wood preparatory to the cutting of the mortises with all the centre bits necessary £200.
3 ditto for mortising with all the various cutters £1100
3 ditto for shaping the shells £700
3 ditto for scoring or cutting the gullets for the straps with all the cutters necessary £150
3 ditto for centering and rounding the lignum vitae after it is converted £200
2 engines for fitting the coaks into the sheaves £150
3 ditto for drilling the holes through the coaks for rivets £150
5 ditto for facing the sheaves £185
4 ditto for finishing the sheaves £75
8 lathes of various sizes with cast iron puppets and chucks for turning dead eyes, trucks etc £270
A complete apparatus for making iron and wood pins £210
TOTAL: £3270[31]

Bentham supported Brunel's request for this further machinery that covered the manufacture of the smaller blocks of 4 to 7in (102 to 178mm) sizes. In June 1803 the Admiralty asked the Navy Board to proceed with this order, adding that Brunel was to continue to be paid his expenses. However, his final payment for the whole project was not to be calculated until the machinery had been in use and the potential savings had been evaluated.[32] In the light of experience being gained from the first set of machines, Brunel incorporated what he described as 'some considerable improvements' in these 'with the approbation of Brigadier General Bentham' in the course of 1803.[33] These modifications seem to have been applied to the two later sets as well. To ensure a steady flow of block parts, he also revised the relative numbers of types of machines.[34] This second order for block-making machines was completed in the summer of 1804. At the end of August that year Bentham was able to report to William Marsden, who had succeeded Nepean in January as first secretary to the Admiralty, that the block-making machinery 'is now capable of supplying the whole of the smaller sizes of

blocks'.[35] By March 1805 the third and final set of machinery for the very largest blocks had been installed and was working[36] (see Endpapers).

Not all the machinery to be used for block-making was designed by Brunel. In 1803 Bentham sought permission to construct three saws of his own design for the Wood Mills. Their frames were timber and the total cost came to £450.[37] In an explanatory letter to Evan Nepean, Bentham wrote:

These engines are intended to be worked by the steam engine, and independently of various other uses to which they may be applicable, they are as it were necessary for the cutting out the wood to the proper scantlings and lengths for shells of blocks, and therefore had it not been that Mr Brunel was apprised of my intention of proposing the introduction of these engines for general purposes, he would have required some such engines as part of the machinery requisite for his part of the business.[38]

These three Bentham machines were a horizontal and a vertical reciprocating saw and a circular saw. It is possible they were among a number that may have been withdrawn from use as early as 1805 while the general was in Russia. Beamish wrote that 'experience had shown that the alternate motion of a saw frame could not be increased beyond a certain number of strokes . . . without endangering the machinery. Brunel therefore abandoned the system and adopted the rotatory. One circular saw of his construction was found to do all the work of twenty-four saws in six frames'.[39]

Although the sets of block-making machinery had been completed and installed by March 1805, Brunel and especially Goodrich were rarely absent from the dockyard over the next few years[40] (Fig 5.2). Staff had to be recruited, trained and made to understand that it was machines and not muscles that would set the pace. Recruiting and discharging staff, establishing wage rates and overseeing the weekly wage payments all remained Goodrich's responsibility until a proper management structure was introduced at the Wood Mills and the Metal Mills.[41] As experience was gained with the machinery and the novelties of mass production, adjustments were made to the layout within the buildings. Other woodworking machines were introduced and there were changes to the steam plant. In July 1805 Bentham sailed for Russia under instruction to look into the possibilities of building warships for the Royal Navy in Russian yards. He was to

Goodrich was finding that the single-acting Sadler engine, where power was applied only on the downward stroke, was not delivering a sufficiently steady rotary motion for the woodworking machinery. He recorded that this engine originally had been used only for draining the dry docks. It had been augmented by the 30hp Boulton and Watt engine in 1800 when Bentham was adding to the load with his woodworking machinery. As Goodrich noted:

> These two steam engines are so arranged by the intervention of proper wheels and shafts, that either of them separately or both of them conjointly, may be connected with all, or with any part of the pumping and Wood Mill machinery. By these means it was intended that in case of necessary repairs, or of extraordinary accidents, one engine might supply the place of the other, or at least in regard to the 12 horse engine, that although it could not do all, it might do the more important part of the work performed by the 30 horse engine, likewise that the force of both engines might be applied when the work required it.[43]

In his diary for Tuesday 24 September 1805, Goodrich noted: 'Busy about the letter to Mr Marsden for the 30 horse engine which with drawings and references are completed this evening ready for sending off'. A growing confidence in his and the dockyard's mechanical engineering abilities is apparent in his next paragraph: 'Suggest also that … I should furnish to the engine maker who may be applied to with more detailed drawings and a list of the articles to be furnished by him in order that he may be agreed with accordingly, as some of the usual articles are dispensed with and some with greater convenience can be supplied by the Dock Yd.'[44]

By 1805 the new block-making machinery had substantially increased the power requirements. As by then all contracts with commercial block-makers had been terminated, it was absolutely imperative that production in the Royal Navy's new factory should be totally reliable. The new water mains were adding a further dimension:

> the raising of fresh water for the supply of the yard, or of the shipping in the basin, or at the jetties, by means of the pipes and reservoir now nearly completed; the throwing of water by means of the same pipes to any part of the yard in case of fire, are all works of great importance dependent on the two steam engines.[45]

Figure 5.2 The Brunel family home in Britain Street, Portsea, demolished in the 1960s. Marc and Sophie lived here with their growing family from 1802 to the summer of 1807 while Marc worked on the Block Mills project. Isambard Kingdom Brunel was born here on 9 April, 1806. (©Anthony Triggs)

be away until December 1807. Simon Goodrich was left in charge in his absence.[42]

With the installation of the final set of Brunel machines, it was apparent that one of the most pressing requirements was to increase the available power by replacing the original 12hp Sadler engine. Before departing for Russia, Bentham had recommended this and Goodrich had been working on these proposals when he had been interrupted by the Saturday morning visit of Nelson and Commissioner Saxton. Later in September, Goodrich wrote to Marsden setting out a very clear case for the new steam engine. As Beamish was later to write,

Goodrich estimated that a new 30 horse engine would cost some £3,000. This included the expenses of two boilers and the relocation of some sawing machinery to make way for the new boiler house. Four days after writing to Marsden, the Navy Board agreed to the purchase of this new engine.[46] For most of October 1805 Goodrich's diary is full of entries such as that for the 8th: 'Busy in the Dock Yard about Steam Engine drawings'.[47] On 13 October he sent six drawings to the Navy Board together with a list of materials. At the end of the month he was in London, and on 28 October he called on Sir John Henslow, one of the two Navy Board surveyors, to discuss the purchase of the engine. In his diary, Goodrich notes: 'Propose to supply him with the copies of the drawings in order that one set may be sent to Whitmore and the other to Murray and Wood that each may propose their terms. He [Henslow] agrees to this.'[48]

At the end of November, Goodrich received from the Navy Board two estimates from the engine manufacturers. His diary for 3 December records some of the problems experienced in dealing with the latter:

Write to the Navy Board and recommend Fenton, Murray and Co. In reference to Mr Whitmore notwithstanding Mr Whitmore Estimate was £189 lower than the other as I was really afraid that Whitmore would do no credit to the engine and that he would disappoint us in time. He had specified no time, Murray had specified six months for the delivery of the materials and also I hope from what has been experienced of the other much more to be depended upon. Beside the various blunders in the Copper Mill Machinery and constant disappointments in time promised, another circumstance contributed materially to set me against Mr W, which was lately discovered, namely that he had made the steam cylinder of the C.M.M engine six inches longer than the stroke of the piston, so that about 1/30 of the whole steam or two horses power was utterly wasted – This was a great want of attention to principle.[49]

Not surprisingly, given this damning evidence, the Navy Board awarded the contract to Fenton, Murray & Co.[50] The new engine was to have a 3ft by 10ft (0.91m x 3m) cylinder and a 17ft (5.2m) diameter flywheel. This firm stuck to the terms of their quotation; by mid-June 1806 the engine parts were ready for inspection in Leeds. On 8 June Mr Linaker, the master millwright at Portsmouth, was sent to inspect these. Presumably all was found to be in order, and by the beginning of August the parts were loaded on a vessel at Hull. Vessel, engine parts and a small team of erectors from the manufacturers arrived at Portsmouth on 19 August. On Friday 22 August, Goodrich noted with satisfaction: 'Go into the Dock Yard and look over some of the engine materials as they are landing and unpacking. All the work seems well executed.'[51]

Although his diary makes no mention of any untoward delays, it was to be late March 1807 before Goodrich was able to record that the new engine 'is now in a forward state'.[52] It was presumably completed soon afterwards, but all was not well with its two new boilers. For much of that summer these were to be plagued by problems of salt forming in them. Finally, in late September, one new iron and one new copper boiler were ordered, and after they were installed the problem seems to have disappeared.[53] The use of both iron and copper boilers clearly reflects uncertainty in the inspector general's department on the merits of the two materials. In 1807 Goodrich estimated that a copper boiler cost four times the £200 cost of an iron one. Nevertheless, he felt the extra cost was justified – 'a copper boiler may last much longer than an iron one, and thereby save the more frequent recurrence of the expense of bricklayers, millwrights and plumbers work attendant upon replacing a boiler'.[54] As an added bonus, Goodrich calculated that the scrap value of a copper boiler was approximately two-thirds of its original cost compared to the 'little or no value' of an iron boiler. These arguments seem to have carried weight with the Navy Board. A report in 1828 lists six copper boilers as having been manufactured in the dockyard since 1816 for the two 30hp steam engines in the Wood Mills and the one 50hp engine in the Metal Mills (Fig 5.3).[55] However, although copper had been used as a boiler material since early in the 18th century, it was much less suited to the Cornish and Lancashire cylindrical boilers introduced from 1812 onwards with their greater heating areas and higher pressures.[56]

The introduction of the Fenton and Murray engine in 1807 (Fig 5.4) alongside the earlier Boulton and Watt engine solved the power requirements of the Block Mills, and it was not until 1830 that a new steam engine needed to be installed.[57] It was probably then that the copper boilers were phased out here.

As resident engineer in these early years, Goodrich played a pivotal role ensuring that the new Portsmouth manufactory was equipped and run as smoothly as

Figure 5.3 'Plan and section of the New Copper Boilers for the 30 Horse Steam Engines at the Wood Mills … 1817.' These boilers operated at very low pressures and tended to have short lives due to the use of impure water. They were known as wagon boilers as their shape suggested a canvas wagon cover. (Science Museum/Science and Society Picture Library, GC, C 215)

possible. His work frequently took him to London, to the Navy Board, to Maudslay's factory and to see Bentham. Later, when Brunel gave up his house in Portsea and moved back to London, Goodrich would often include him in his visits to the capital. Maudslay and Bentham both made numbers of trips to Portsmouth during the construction phase of the Block Mills. These continued during the early years of production when practical experience sometimes suggested modifications to the layout or to the machinery itself. Goodrich's diary is our chief source of information, and chronicles the frustrations as well as the successes.

Although the block-making machinery was in many ways the most complex of all the machinery to be installed in the building, Brunel's attention to the details of its design, combined with Maudslay's manufacturing skills, seems to have resulted in its causing the fewest problems. The same could not be said of some of the other machines, especially the sawing machinery, and Goodrich's diary gives fascinating glimpses of the not-always-smooth relations with Marc Brunel. Many of the problems here stemmed from the latter's proprietorial interest in the project and his unwritten assumption that he could on occasion use the building as a test-bed for his own ideas. Goodrich's

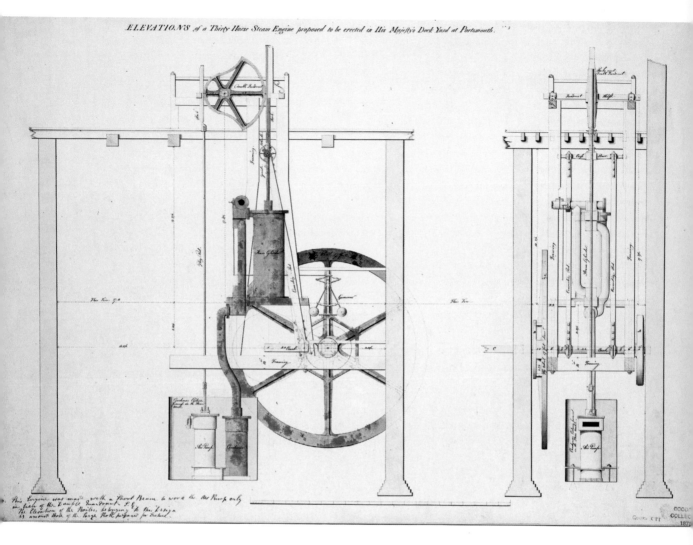

Figure 5.4 The Fenton and Murray engine installed in 1807. This was designed by Simon Goodrich in 1805, following the table-engine pattern of the earlier Sadler design. Its compact layout, compared to a beam engine, was probably crucial to its successful installation in the restricted space of the existing engine house. As built, the differential quadrant rack mechanism for driving the condenser air pump was changed to a simple half-beam. The flywheel had a diameter of 17 ft (5.1m). (Science Museum/Science and Society Picture Library, GC, C 77)

diary entry for 15 August 1805 gives an indication of how the system was supposed to work. He noted:

Mr Brunel called at the Office yesterday. Left several papers stating the present state of the woodmills and what is further wanted. He also leaves the drawing for a new crank saw for cross-cutting on a very simple plan. Meet Mr Brunel this morning at Maudslays. Look over his papers. Make some observations upon them and leave them to him to copy and to return them to me dated and signed.

From this it is clear that, as might be expected, Goodrich had to approve the final drawings on Bentham's behalf before Maudslay could undertake the work. However, 'Mr Brunel in the course of conversation expressed the wish to make trial of his patent circular saw at the Woodmills privately on his own account and at his own expense and wanted to know if I could do anything in it for him. I said that I could do nothing in it but that he might apply if he pleased to the Admiralty or Navy Board.'[58]

This Brunel did. On 2 September he saw Goodrich and told him that the Admiralty was writing to Commissioner Saxton granting Brunel permission to try his saw at the Wood Mills 'and to allow him such assistance as he might require'.[59] He wasted no time. Later that month Goodrich records: 'Go into the Dock Yard, see Brunel's cross-cutting horizontal reciprocating saw at work upon Lignum Vitae. He has been long bringing it to bear. It seems likely to answer.'[60] Just over a fortnight later, Goodrich saw 'Brunel's Patent Saw tried at the Woodmills. It does not answer well.' The next day he recorded: 'At the Woodmills, consulting with Maudslay and Brunel about the cross-cutting circular saw for lignum vitae. Brunel has not, after long and many trials, brought the cross-cutting saw to bear.'[61] By the following June, Brunel was ready to try again. Goodrich was unamused to visit the Wood Mills and find that:

Brunel has also got another large Circular Saw sent down to be tried this the third . . . without any reference to me or I believe anyone else [he] has had his large circular saw apparatus moved down from the third floor of the North Wood Mill Building where it was first fixed to try it, into the Lower Floor of the same building where it has again been put to work and is very much in the way.[62]

Some sort of rapprochement may have been attempted later that month between the two men, for Goodrich records that on Sunday 29 June he 'spent evening at Mr Brunels'.[63]

However, if there was an understanding reached then, it was very short-lived. On 8 August 1806 Goodrich went into the Block Mills and found that Brunel was still:

taking down, altering and making new things without reference or consultation tho' I am on the spot. I am apprehensive in many cases all authority is exceeded and in many others unnecessary expenses incurred. How to check it without quarrelling is a difficult matter . . . But it is now to be suspected that Brunel is preparing for erecting a manufactory on his own account that he makes . . . all the experiments he can

here in subservience to his views, and that he may wish to hang on as long as he can here whilst he is preparing his plans and drawings on his other account [a reference to his proposed sawmill at Battersea].[64]

Four days later Goodrich steeled himself to confront Brunel and his methods of working. Goodrich's diary records:

Come to an explanation with Brunel on the propriety of no new work or considerable alterations of old, being put in hand without my being apprised and consulted about it in order to form some opinion of the advantages of the measure, as well as to procure the requisite authority for it. He did not yield the point with a good grace at first by words, but his conduct afterwards in calling upon me and offering explanations of several things was more to the purpose and I hope the hint will do some good.[65]

This meeting had little lasting effect. In late October that year:

Brunel meets me at the Wood Mills and makes a violent and as I think unjust attack on Burr and same attack on myself in consequence of two men having been entered [on the books] during his absence without his having been consulted about it. Although he had absented himself for three weeks without any communication to me . . . or without my knowing when he intended to return . . . He urges many things against Burr . . . and insists upon that a nail ought not to be driven without his consent. I repress my vexation at his unreasonable and unfair insinuations and assure him that I will not suffer Burr to do anything without his concurrence and that I will do nothing myself relative to the Wood Mills, when I can consistently with my public duty, without consulting him, so long as he is concerned in the work here.[66]

The last sentence hints at the nub of the problem – the lack of clearly defined roles for the principal players. Brunel was still being paid only a small daily attendance rate. The financial reward for his inventions was to be calculated on the annual production savings of his new machinery once it had all been installed. This gave him every incentive to refine both the machines and the methods of operation – which had no doubt been central to Bentham's thinking when he originally devised the contract. Brunel could also point to the Admiralty support of September 1805 for his being allowed to try out his machinery in the Block Mills.[67] Goodrich, as a salaried official, was concerned not just with the efficient running of the machinery and production process, but also with the need to stay within accepted government financial and procurement guidelines.

This seems to have been the last serious difference of opinion between Goodrich and Brunel. By then the Block Mills were over the worst teething problems and the production rate was increasing as the workforce expanded and acquired new skills. But Brunel's thoughts were also turning to the construction of his own sawmill at Battersea, a point noted by Goodrich the following March: 'Brunel seems much taken up with his new schemes and hangs in here without doing much good'.[68]

In the summer of 1807 Brunel sold his Portsea house and moved his family to Lindsey Row, Chelsea. His visits to Portsmouth became correspondingly less frequent, although he continued to receive his attendance allowance. Not until September 1808 did Bentham, back from his abortive Russian trip, advise that Brunel was no longer needed at Portsmouth.[69] The disagreements between Goodrich and Brunel were not long-lasting, and in later years they seem to have maintained a cordial relationship.

In supervising the work on the Block Mills, Goodrich had many other calls on his time and his patience apart from Brunel. The building work was the responsibility of the dockyard bricklayers and joiners. This does not seem to have been a problem, apart from a partial collapse of the brick piers of the vaults in 1802 (see p 40). This workforce was in any event under the direct supervision of the dockyard staff and the two architects, first Samuel Bunce, then Edward Holl. However, the construction and installation of all the machinery was generally the preserve of the various manufacturers who sent their own staff to provide the nucleus of a skilled labour force. These would be augmented as necessary by local men. In November 1805 Goodrich recorded in his diary: 'Endeavour to settle with Maudslay's men here about their working more time for a day's work. They are refractory, but I leave the matter to Maudslay and Brunel to settle as long as they are under Maudslay. Their wages are rather low so they want to make it up in time.'[70] Surprisingly, this seems to have been a problem limited to Maudslay's workmen.

As the machinery was installed under the supervision of Goodrich, Brunel and Bentham, workers had to be found and trained to operate it. At first, this presented a number of problems, both on account of the lack of skilled staff and on their initial terms of employment. As already mentioned, Brunel's original agreement with the Admiralty had stipulated that the financial reward for his invention and for the time spent installing the machinery was to be a sum equal to the saving made in one year by its use. Such an arrangement had obvious attractions to the Admiralty, for it put the onus for the success of the project firmly on the inventor. Brunel was well aware that the size of his reward would depend directly on the number of blocks that the machinery could manufacture in one year's operation. This in turn depended on the number of capable workmen employed in the Block Mills. Once the first machinery started to arrive in March 1803, this became a more pressing problem, for it was also Brunel's responsibility to recruit the workmen for his new machines. Terms of employment for the steam-engine operators, stokers, pump operatives and those employed on Bentham's own woodworking machinery lay with the normal dockyard recruitment and employment methods, although these men seem to have worked directly to Bentham's own supervisory staff. Such a system had the potential for trouble, particularly when applied to sets of workmen in the same building, each dependent on the other.

Brunel could offer his workmen no security of tenure. As he wrote to Bentham later that year: 'Being entirely unacquainted [with the workmen] and fearful of their not being continued in that business, I cannot promise any encouragement such as to induce good workmen to leave their work.'[71] This problem was to dog Brunel for the next few years. Thus in October 1803, when asked for an estimate of the number of blocks that his first set of machines could supply in the next four weeks, he could only reply:

that from the want of four block-makers, it would be impossible for him to form an estimate . . . I cannot therefore answer but for what can be done by six labourers and two house carpenters, who, if at work without interruption, at the rate of nine hours and a half per day, will be able to make in six days or a week one thousand.[72]

In a further and more despondent note in January 1805, Brunel wrote to Bentham:

The block-making has hitherto been managed so very badly, that it is not possible to ascertain exactly the price of every part, so as to determine the extent of the piecework of the labourers. This bad management is entirely owing to the want of a steam engine keeper conversant with its parts, and capable of foreseeing accidents and guarding against them . . . The present keepers are stopped by the least difficulty, and cannot point out the cause. The person who gives the orders for pumping [the reservoir] is the manager of the steam engine. Owing to his absolute ignorance, particularly in the management of the steam engine, the keepers are not able to point out any defects, and keep on until it stops entirely.[73]

There may well be an element of exaggeration here. However, with the imminent arrival of the final set of block-making machines, there was clearly a need to integrate the workforce in the building and to sort out a coherent chain of command. No doubt spurred by Brunel's letter of complaint about the inadequacies of the engine keepers, Simon Goodrich the following month wrote to Whitmore of Birmingham, asking if the firm could recommend a good engine-keeper 'to take charge and management of the steam engines'.[74] Goodrich did not rule out finding a suitable man at Portsmouth, but it is an indication of the lack of skilled labour that he felt it necessary to look as far afield as Birmingham. Early in September 1805 Goodrich spent some time devising a

Figure 5.5 The stoke hole of the Boulton and Watt boiler house in 2004. The base of the chimney is in the centre. Although there are no specific references in any of the early documents to stokers, the boiler-room staff were crucial to the efficient running of the engines. (EH, AA 042393)

new wage structure for scavel-men and labourers at the Block Mills, and in identifying individuals he felt were able to take on some of the more responsible tasks, such as engine keepers. Although it is not recorded, Goodrich must have also looked at the overall management. After this exercise, labour problems seem to have diminished.[75] In part, the regularisation of wages must have helped, but the growing experience of the workforce would have made a major contribution. Curiously, there is little in the records relating to the establishment of the Wood Mills to suggest that the project suffered from the sorts of labour problems that were being engendered in the dockyards by Bentham's wider labour reforms.[76] This, however, may reflect the novelty of a project with no long-established labour practices (Fig 5.5).

Brunel's reference to a 9½ hour day for the workforce would present no problems in the long summer days, but winter was a different matter. It cannot be a coincidence that in early September 1805 Goodrich was 'preparing a letter about lamps for the Wood Mills' (Figs 5.6 and 5.7). He calculated that he would need some four dozen. In an environment full of sawdust, wood shavings and belt-operated machinery, with none of the safety guards that are now the norm, this was a potential conflagration in the making unless stringent precautions were taken. The amount of chippings created by the shaping machines in particular must have been prodigious. Farey noted in Rees that Bentham encouraged the operatives to take care of their machines, and said in the long run it saved money on replacing worn parts. The need for continual cleanliness might also be the reason for the numbers of boys employed. The only production processes in the royal dockyards that presented similar hazards were the naval roperies. In these, working patterns followed daylight hours, and no lights seem to have been installed until the coming of electricity in the 20th century.

However, in 1804 Goodrich had travelled north to Sunderland to visit John Grimshaw, whose commercial rope-yard was considered to be the most modern in Britain.[77] There he evidently saw lanterns designed by John Grimshaw especially for use in a ropery, and it was to these that he turned in the autumn of 1805. His letter to the Navy Board suggested they obtain a sample as a pattern; Goodrich noted the lantern's convenience and safety and 'of the advantages of getting as much work as possible from a given Capital expended'. He also enclosed an estimate from Grimshaw offering to supply these at

16s 6d each, including the burners.[78] In the event, the Navy Board seems to have ordered the four dozen from Sunderland, and they were delivered to Portsmouth in mid-November. So successful were they that a further 72 were bought for the Wood Mills the following July.[79]

With the Block Mills machinery bedded in, lanterns for winter working installed and the workforce gaining in confidence and experience, Burr felt able to write to the Navy Board in November 1807 confirming that the Wood Mills 'would now be able to answer all demands'.[80]

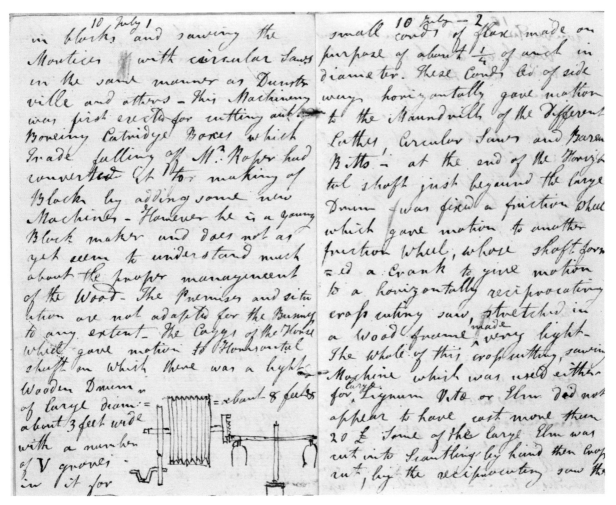

Figures 5.6 and 5.7 Simon Goodrich was involved in every aspect of the operation of the Block Mills, as we see from entries in his diary. In those entries for July 1806, for example, he was concerned with the supply of 'Six Dozen Lamp Lanterns to be provided for the Wood Mills' from Mr Grimshaw. He also comments, rather disparagingly, on the horse-wheel-driven block-making machinery he has viewed at Mr Roper's manufactory in Houndsditch. (Science Museum/Science and Society Picture Library, GC, Book 14, 9.7.1806 and 10.7.1806)

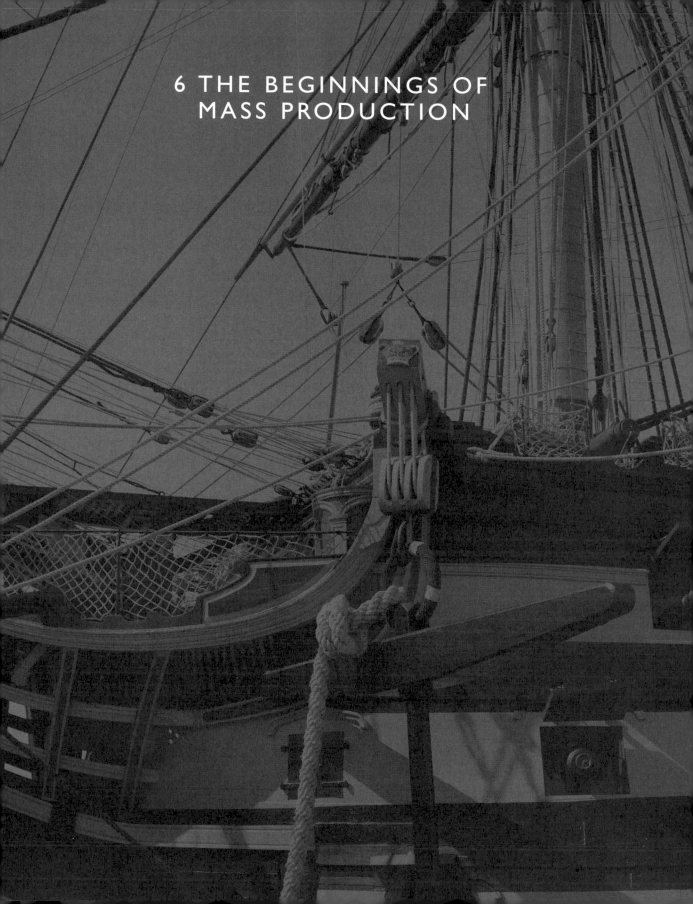

6 THE BEGINNINGS OF MASS PRODUCTION

The success of the Block Mills was crucial to the reputations of both Brunel and Bentham. To a certain extent, the delays to the project had caused a measure of criticism and concern to both Admiralty and Navy Boards. These delays were partly attributable to the novelty and complexity of the whole undertaking. However, the Navy Board also blamed Brunel for making numerous alterations and additions as the project proceeded. He, in turn, justified these by pointing out that the growing requirements of an expanding fleet were forcing an increase in production targets. Brunel had based his figures on the demands of the navy between 1797 and 1801. By the time construction of the Block Mills was well under way, he 'found it necessary to give such a disposition to the building and machinery so as to enable it to supply a much greater proportion of the work than was at first calculated'.[1]

The immediate practical consequences of delays in the project lay in the need to maintain a supply of blocks for the navy. Taylor at Southampton was the largest commercial manufacturer, followed by Dunsterville at Plymouth. In 1803 Taylor had his contract cancelled and renewed only on a short term basis; between then and 1805 the contract had to be renegotiated four times. As the firm expected to go out of business when it finally lost the Navy Board contracts, this made for a very uncomfortable relationship.[2] Consideration was even given by Bentham in 1803 to purchasing some of the Dunsterville machinery as an interim solution, but this idea was abandoned.[3]

Nevertheless, as the various problems were overcome, Brunel and Goodrich were able gradually to step up production. By the end of August 1804 Bentham was able to report to the Admiralty that the block-making machinery 'is now capable of supplying the whole of the smaller sizes of Blocks'.[4] By the middle of February 1805, Bentham noted that production had reached a total of around 50,000 blocks.[5] In early November 1806 Brunel estimated that his machinery by then had produced a total of 'upwards of 160,000 blocks' for the Royal Navy.[6] In 1807 the original Sadler table engine was replaced by a new 30hp Murray and Wood beam engine. The additional power and reliability probably helped Brunel to confirm in September that by mid-October the block-making machinery would be capable of supplying 'all the Blocks for the Navy'.[7] The only obstacle appeared to be the spasmodic supply of metal coaks from the foundry. In September, Brunel had complained to Goodrich that this

was a problem of some long standing and was preventing orders being fulfilled – 'there were no coaks left today at noon'. The foundry foreman informed Brunel that the problem was staff shortage.[8] The next month Brunel complained again, noting that Burr arranged for the coaks to be collected 'as soon as they are fit for delivery. The irregularity of supplies causes a great irregularity in the work at the mill, for the men being obliged to alter frequently their engines, cannot make their wages upon piece-work, and the orders cannot be executed'.[9] Like other teething problems, the supply problems of coaks seem to have been overcome, and by 1808 the Block Mills achieved an annual output of 130,000 blocks.[10] The age of machine-produced mass production had finally arrived.

Although a great deal is known about the Brunel machinery and the purpose and operation of each individual machine, much less is known about how the machinery was originally arranged within the building. Between them, Brunel, Bentham and Goodrich were in effect establishing the world's first factory where power-driven machine tools set the pace, dictated the layout and carried out nearly all the manufacturing processes. Inevitably, given the pioneering nature of the enterprise, there are documentary references to modifications being made as experience accumulated. However, at no stage are any of the principal players known to have written down a description of the actual internal layout of the Block Mills, described the positions of individual machines or indicated precisely how the various stages of production dovetailed with each other.

The three main parts of a block, the shell, the sheave or pulley wheel, and the pin for holding the latter in the shell, are shown in Figure 6.1. When Brunel had originally turned his thoughts to the possibilities of manufacturing blocks, his first task had been to identify the various stages of manufacture of each of their component parts. His next and most difficult was to design a series of machines that could undertake these individual stages of manufacture. Each machine had to be capable of accurate repetitive work, and by simple adjustment of cutters, drills and mortise chisels to cope with batches of a variety of different sized block components. Such accuracy had the further substantial benefit of allowing the interchangeability of parts – an impossibility with the largely hand-crafted blocks then in use. This need for accuracy and precision, as well as strength and durability to cope with the force of steam power, led to Brunel and Maudslay making the machine

75

Figure 6.1 The various stages of manufacture of block shells (top), the sheaves (centre) and the final assembly of the block (bottom). (From Gilbert 1965, 11, Figs 6, 7 & 8, Science Museum/Science and Society Picture Library)

tools of all-metal construction. Although the machine operators required some skills to work the machinery, these were deliberately kept to the minimum to lessen the chances of operator error and to allow the employment of semi-skilled labour. Mostly their tasks were limited to clamping the material to the machines, using adjustable guides and stops that were set for particular sizes and types of block production. Once the material had been fixed in position, the operator then worked the controls, again largely pre-set, to start the machine and bring the material into contact with the various types of tools. Although it is not specifically recorded, adjusting the settings of the machines to cater for batches of different sizes and types of blocks was almost certainly the responsibility of the foremen. After completion of the individual components, these were brought together for final hand-assembly.

All the timber elements of the blocks were processed within the building. However, the metal pins and the bell-metal coaks, inserted in the centres of the sheaves as bearings for the pins, were manufactured elsewhere, although the pins were finished and polished on site (Figs 6.2, 6.3 and 6.4). The 45 block-making machines were of 22 kinds, each with a specific task. Within this overall total were three different sized sets of machines to cater for the variety of sizes of blocks required by the fleet. By adjusting the settings on these groups of machines and the saws, the machinery could produce over 200 sizes and types of pulley blocks.[11] Fig 6.5 shows the various processes as a flow chart.

Figure 6.2 A pin-turning lathe, used for the turning of the pin blanks before polishing. Like all the block-making machinery, these lathes could be adjusted and set for different sized pins. For single blocks, these varied from $\frac{1}{2}$ in $\times$ $3\frac{1}{4}$ in to $2\frac{1}{4}$ in $\times$ 21in (13mm $\times$ 83mm to 57mm $\times$ 533mm). (Science Museum/Science and Society Picture Library, GC, C 40)

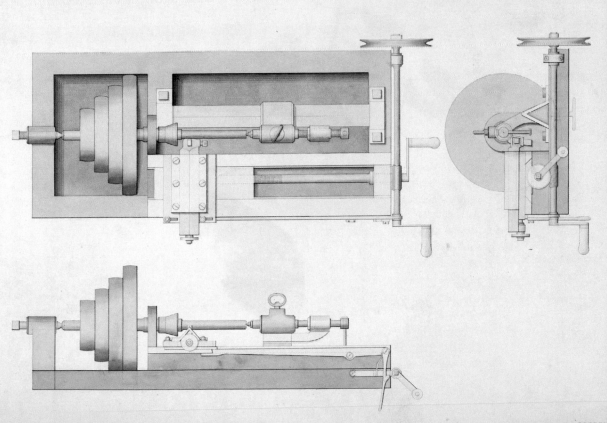

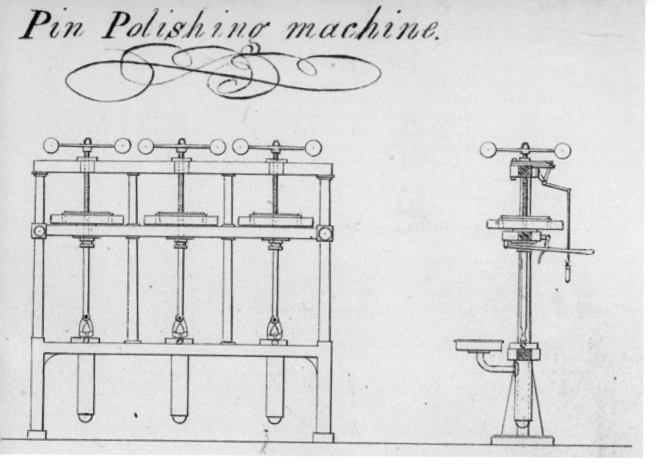

Pin Polishing machine.

Figure 6.3 (above)
Brunel's sketchbook drawing of pin-polishing machines. The pins were made from wrought iron. (© National Maritime Museum, London, MS 85, Brunel's sketchbook)

Figure 6.4 (right)
Pin-polishing machines in the Block Mills late in the 19th century. Pins were given a highly polished and burnished finish by being rotated slowly between hardened steel dies in oil. By the time of this photograph, the machines had become obsolete and were disused. Henry Roland's illustrations from his article about changes in machine-shop practice during the nineteenth century are the only nineteenth-century photographs known of the interior of the Block Mills. (From Roland 1899, 53)

Figure 6.5 (opposite) Flow chart of the sequence of production of the component parts of a block. (EH, based on Cooper 1981–2, 31)

SLICE OF LIGNUM
VITAE LOG CUT BY
CONVERTING SAW

BLANK SHEAVE
CUT OUT AND BORED
BY THE ROUNDING SAW

RECESS CUT BY
COAKING ENGINE

GUN-METAL COAK
INSERTED BY HAND

COPPER RIVETS
INSERTED BY HAND
IF NECESSARY

RIVETING HAMMER
SETS COAK AND RIVETS

BROACHING ENGINE
REAMS HOLE TO SIZE

SHEAVE FINISHED IN
FACE-TURNING LATHE

IRON PIN
HAND-SWAGED
IN SMITHY

MACHINED IN
PIN-TURNING
LATHE

FINISHED IN
PIN-POLISHING
MACHINE

BLOCK CUT FROM
AN ELMWOOD LOG
BY CONVERTING SAW

HOLES DRILLED BY
BORING MACHINE

SLOTS CUT IN
MORTISING MACHINE

SHELL ROUGHLY SHAPED
BY CORNER SAW

COMPLETED BY
SHAPING ENGINE

SCORING ENGINE
CUTS GROOVES
FOR ROPE

SHELL HAND-FINISHED
WITH A SPOKESHAVE

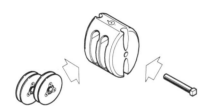

PULLEY BLOCK FINAL ASSEMBLY BY HAND:
THE GROOVES CAST ON THE INSIDES OF THE COAKS ARE FILLED WITH GREASE,
THE IRON PIN IS INSERTED THROUGH THE PINHOLES OF THE SHELL AND SHEAVES,
THEN HAMMERED UNTIL THE SQUARE HEAD BITES INTO THE SHELL TO HOLD IT FAST.

The shell of a block was always manufactured from elm wood. The elm was first cut into lengths either by a circular saw or, if large, by a reciprocating saw. The lengths of timber were then placed on a sawbench and fed through a rip-saw to square their sides. These lengths were then cross-cut to the correct sizes for particular blocks, and the rectangular blocks of elm were taken from the sawmill to the first of the specialised block-making machines. These were the boring machines that drilled the holes (Fig 6.6). One small one was in the centre of the face of the timber block to receive the pin on which the sheave or pulley wheel would turn. The other and larger hole (or holes, if multi-sheaved blocks were to be made) was towards the top of the side of the block. This latter hole formed the guide for the next stage of manufacturing. This took place on the mortising machine which enlarged the hole into a slot that would ultimately house the sheave (Figs 6.7 and 6.8). The shell was then taken to a corner-saw that, as its name implies, cut off the corners of the block (Fig 6.9). Ten blocks at a time were then clamped to a shaping machine which revolved them against a gouge that cut them to their final shape (Figs 6.10 and 6.11). Pairs of shells were then attached to a table on a scoring machine that cut the external grooves or scores. These scores held the strop rope that was spliced around the shell and which ultimately held the block in its position on board ship[12] (Figs 6.12, 6.13 and 6.14). The complete shell was probably varnished at this stage.

The sheave or pulley wheel that formed the revolving heart of the block was manufactured from lignum vitae, a tropical wood from South America that is one of the hardest and most stable of all timbers. Logs of lignum vitae were cut into slices on one of three saws or converting machines (Figs 6.15 and 6.16). These slices were then fixed to a rounding machine or rounding saw, which made the slices absolutely circular (Fig 6.17). At the same time the machine bored a hole through the centre for the coak or bearing for the pin on which the sheave would eventually revolve. The coak was cast from bell metal for durability and to avoid corrosion, and incorporated an internal spiral groove to hold lubricating grease. It came in two parts, each with three lobes or ears. The disc of wood of the part-formed sheave was next fixed to a coaking machine which milled three recesses on each side of the disc to receive the ears of the two parts of the coak (Figs 6.18 and 6.19). The latter were then placed into the disc on opposite sides, holes were drilled through the ears and the disc, and the whole assembly of disc and coak was held together by wire

pins riveted through the three holes (Fig 6.20). Next a broaching machine bored out the coaks, ensuring that they were cylindrical and concentric with the rim of the sheave (Fig 6.21). The final stage of production of the sheave saw it fixed on a face-turning lathe that ensured that both faces were smooth. The last part of the operation was to cut a groove in the rim for the rope (Fig 6.22).

The third main component of the block was its iron pin. This was forged with one end left square to bite into the shell and hold the pin secure to prevent it rotating. The pins were not manufactured in the Block Mills. They arrived in a semi-finished state, needing only to be turned smooth in a pin-turning lathe and then burnished in a pin-polishing machine (see Figs 6.2, 6.3 and 6.4). Farey, writing in Rees's *Cyclopaedia*, (the only source to say so), noted that the pins were finally tinned to prevent rusting. The final part of the production process was to assemble the shell, sheave and pin by hand.

This very simplified outline of the various processes does not do justice to the ingenuity of some of the more complex machines that operated on a semi-automatic basis once put in motion. The shaping engines, for example, were able to swivel all 10 shells to ensure that all their sides came into contact with the gouges. Similarly, the scoring machines had the shell-holders fixed to a table that rotated through 180 degrees so that both ends of the shells could be scored. The coaking machine, which was designed to cut the recesses on both sides of the sheave to receive the ears of the coak, was perhaps the most complex of all:

The sheave is held internally by an expanding arbour [*sic*] made of three segments of a ring, which are forced apart by drawing them into a tapered plug . . . The sheave is secured below the cutter spindle to a table, which is moved away from the axis with the result that a recess is milled in the sheave to a depth and extent determined by stops. The table is equipped with an indexing mechanism by which the sheave is rotated through 120 degrees for the next cut.[13]

The expanding arbor for some time was thought to have been invented by Brunel, but more recent research has shown that he had been anticipated in it by Leonardo da Vinci. However, it is thought that Brunel was the first to design and use a cone clutch in the mortising machines. Such a clutch allowed an operator to disengage the machine from the drive and stop it without destroying the momentum of the flywheel.[14]

Figure 6.6 (above and right) Boring machines in use in the Block Mills in the 1890s. In a single operation these drilled the holes in the solid elm blocks for both the sheave pin and the mortise chisels. Adjustable stops located the block in position. The clamp and gripping pad holding it had sharp points and a sharp-edged raised ring which incised location points in the timber for late stages of machining. The revolving boring bits were mounted on two adjustable slides at right angles to each other. Handles were used to move these, thus forcing the bits through the wood. Adjustable stops controlled the travel. (From Roland 1899, 56)

Figure 6.7 A mortising machine. The vertical sliding frame and two chisels for double blocks can be seen clearly at the left end. In operation, the blocks were positioned using the location marks incised on them earlier by the boring machine, and clamped securely in a substantial metal frame. This frame slid on guides and could be moved by a fixed worm on which was a threaded bush attached to the machine frame. Attached to this bush was a ratchet, operated by a pawl mechanism driven by a cam on the drive axis. Turning the threaded bush by a handle moved the frame and block relative to the mortise chisels to adjust them at the start of the cut. Once the correct length of mortise slot had been cut, an adjustable automatic device threw the pawl out of gear and stopped the frame. A cone clutch allowed the main flywheel to continue running while the operator replaced the block. (From Brewster c1811, plate LVIII, Science Museum/Science and Society Picture Library)

Figure 6.8 One of the mortising machines in use in the 1890s. In the foreground is a pile of blocks awaiting their mortise slots. An operator using the smallest of the three sizes of mortising machines could machine an average of just under one 6in (152mm) block every minute. (From Roland 1899, 56)

Figure 6.9 A Brunel corner-saw which is still *in situ* in the Block Mills. As its name implies, this is a circular saw with an angled work table to allow the corners to be cut from the rectangular block shells after mortising. Wooden packing boards were originally provided to adjust the cut to the particular size of blocks. This saw has a Bentham-type parallel-rule adjustable fence for the same purpose, indicating the close collaboration between Brunel, Bentham and Maudslay.
(© Crown copyright. NMR, MPBW J371-2-68)

M. J.Brunel Invent! J.Farey Del!

H. Maudslay Fecit

Eng.by J.Mollat Edin!

Figure 6.10 A shaping machine, used to produce the curved outer faces of the block. The heart of the machine was two rings attached to a central shaft. Ten blocks were fixed between the rings, around their circumference, by clamps which had spikes and rings to locate the indents on the shells formed earlier on the boring machine. One ring had a mechanism for rotating the blocks between cuts. The cutting tool was a hollow gouge clamped in a holder on a slide. As the operator pressed this towards the revolving rings, it followed a curved former. By swinging the gouge holder from side to side against the latter, the two motions generated the curved shape of the block. One ring had a mechanism for rotating the blocks between cuts. To rotate these simultaneously to present a new face to be cut, a large bevel gear on the main shaft drove small bevel gears on shafts radiating out to the blocks. These shafts had small worm-wheels that meshed with gears attached to the clamps that held the blocks. To make the first cut, the rings were secured to each other and rotated, carrying the block with them. Then the operator locked the large bevel gear so it could not move, unlocked the rings and rotated them on the shaft. This caused the small bevels to revolve around the locked bevel and rotate the shafts, worms and block shells in their clamps. This process had to be repeated four times to rotate the shells through 90 degrees. The large bevel was then unlocked, but before a new face could be machined, a former with a different curve had to be positioned to guide the gouge. After this face was cut the process was repeated until the blocks were fully machined. (From Brewster *c*1811, plate LIX, Science Museum/Science and Society Picture Library)

Figure 6.11 (above)
A shaping machine in use in the 1890s. As with all the block-making machines, Brunel took great care to make them simple to use. Although the operation of the shaping machine was complex, once it had been set up for a particular size of block, all the operator had to do was to clamp these in place, machine them and unload them. (From Roland 1899, 52)

Figure 6.12 (right)
A Maudslay model of a scoring machine. This cut the score round the body of the block to seat the strop rope which attached it to the rigging. The score was deepest at the ends of the block, tapering to nothing where it crossed the pin hole. This shows two blocks clamped in position with the cutter wheels poised to cut the grooves for the strop ropes. The tapered groove can be clearly seen on the top of the completed block at the foot of the machine on the right (© National Maritime Museum, London)

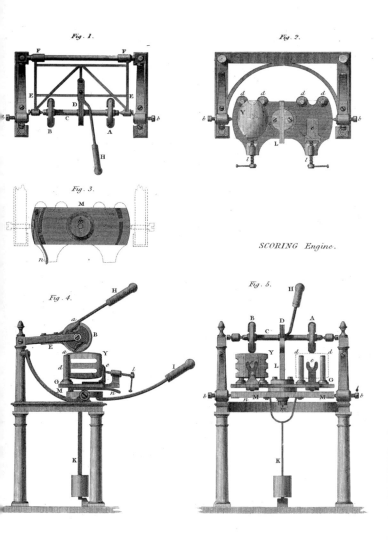

Figure 6.13 The scoring machine as depicted in Rees's *Cyclopaedia* (1812). Two blocks at a time were clamped against stops on a rocking table. The operator used one handle to rock the table and a second one to press a frame holding revolving cutters against a profile cam fixed to the table. This raised the cutters over the pinholes and lowered them as they reached the ends of the blocks. To cut the other halves of these sides of the shell, the table was turned 180 degrees and the process repeated. The blocks were then removed and repositioned with their uncut faces uppermost to allow a repetition of the cutting operations.

Figure 6.14 A model of a scoring machine clearly showing the strop-rope groove being formed by the cutter wheel. (From Gilbert 1965, 28, Fig 24, Science Museum/Science and Society Picture Library)

Figure 6.15 (above) The great lignum vitae saw in use in 1965. This cut the lignum vitae blanks for the sheaves. (© Crown copyright. NMR, MPBW J341-6-65)

Figure 6.16 (right) The lignum vitae saw today. This is one of only two Brunel machines to remain in its original position in the building. The belt-driven horizontal circular saw can be seen on its swinging arm. Below, the lignum vitae log is secured in a chuck on a vertical sliding frame. The operator could raise the log by means of a geared lead screw until the required thickness protruded above the saw blade. The latter was then swung across the log. Simultaneously, the operator turned a crank that rotated the chuck and log, allowing the blade to cut right round the circumference of the wood, and ensure a parallel thickness of the slice. (EH, AA 042414)

Figure 6.17 A rounding saw for truing-up the sheave blank. In the centre is the bit that bored a hole through the middle of the sheave in preparation for the insertion of the bell-metal coak. (From Gilbert 1965, 30, Fig 27, Science Museum/Science and Society Picture Library)

Figure 6.18 The smaller coaking machine. Mounted on this is a part-formed sheave about to have the three recesses milled for the 'ears' of the coak. (From Gilbert 1965, 31, Fig 29, Science Museum/Science and Society Picture Library)

Figure 6.19 Both coaking machines in use in the Block Mills in the 1890s. These milled the recesses on both sides of the sheave that would contain the coak or metal bearing on which the sheave revolved. The heart of the smaller machine, to the left, was a work table which could be moved sideways and also indexed round in steps of 120 degrees. The sheave was clamped to this by means of an expanding collet chuck that locked into the bore of the sheave. Above was a vertical milling spindle with a three-bladed cutter. This was lowered on top of the bore to the required thickness of the coak. The table was then swung sideways against a stop, allowing the cutters to machine one coak ear. By repeating the operation, and indexing the table through 120 degrees, the remaining two ears could be machined. The sheave was then unclamped and turned over. At this point, a spring-loaded button, the diameter of the ear of the coak, rose up from the table and engaged one of the already formed ears. This simple but ingenious mechanism ensured that the ears of the coak and ring were opposite each other for the later riveting.

In the larger machine to the right, the milling spindle was fixed to one side of a hinged frame rather like a vertical door hinge, the other side of which was secured to the frame of the machine. The sheave was fixed by an expanding collet to a work table which was made to rise and fall by a treadle mechanism to achieve the correct depth of cut and to lower the sheave out of the way when the job was finished.

The milling spindle was fitted with a pin which ran round the inside of a metal former cut to the profile of the face of the coak to be inset into the sheave. The milling cutter followed this movement, excavating the wood as it did so. (From Roland 1899, 52)

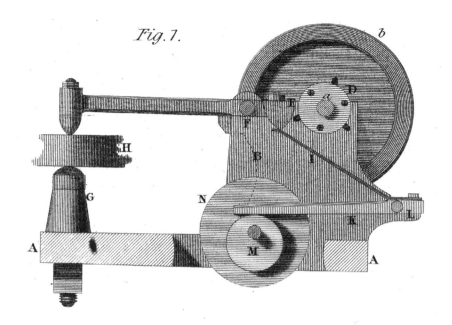

Fig. 1.

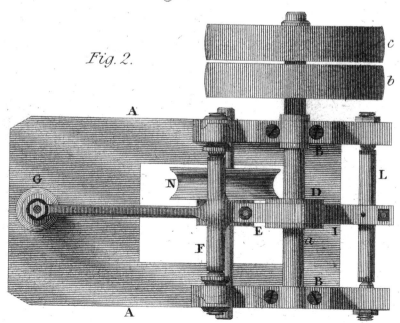

Riveting Hammer.

Fig. 2.

Figure 6.20 Riveting hammer from Rees's *Cyclopaedia* (1812). 'H' is the sheave in position for the hammer to secure the coak. In essence, this was a small tilt hammer, the head raised by a three-lobed cam and driven down by a strong adjustable spring under the tail of the hammer. According to Lady Bentham, the riveting together of the two halves of the coak was originally done by hand, but the quality was not consistent, so her husband designed this machine.

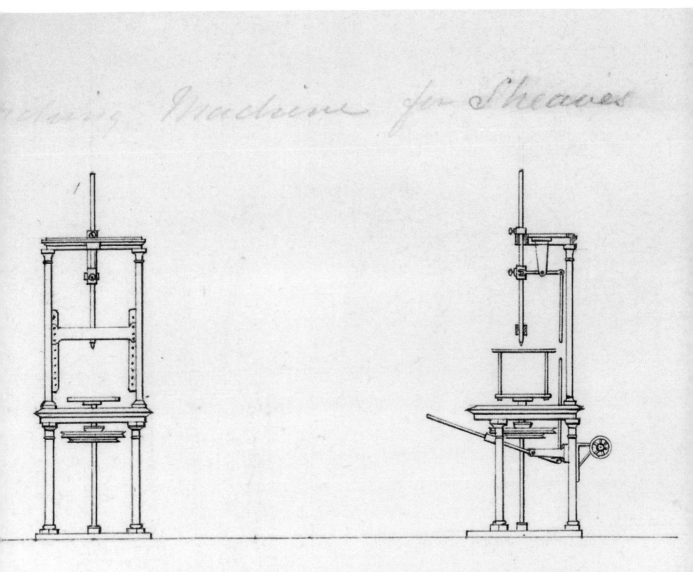

Figure 6.21 Brunel's sketch of the broaching machine that was used to ensure that the coak was properly positioned within the centre of the sheave, and the bore of the latter was smooth and cylindrical. The sheave was placed on a horizontal plate with a central hole attached to a hollow vertical spindle driven by a belt from the line shafting. The broach itself was a smooth cylinder that fitted the bore of the revolving spindle and had a small cutter projecting from it. This was located over the horizontal plate and could be raised and lowered by the operator. The bottom of the broach was pushed through the sheave into the lower spindle and the sheave was then clamped. As the lower table revolved and the broach was forced down through the hole in the coak, the interior was finished off true. To cater for the variety of pin sizes, a suite of table spindles, or possibly a variety of bushes, and boring bars would have been required. (© National Maritime Museum, London, Brunel's sketch book)

Fig. 2.

Figure 6.22 A face-turning lathe used for the final part of the sheave production. This ensured that both faces of the sheave were smooth and the rim had a groove for the rope. The sheave (A) was fixed to a lathe chuck in same way as on the coaking machine. The lower half of the compound slide-rest (a) moved the tool into position so that it could begin cutting across the face of the sheave towards its rim. Once the metal centre of the coak had been machined, the operator moved the drive belt to a smaller pulley on the top slide screw, allowing it to turn faster for facing the wood of the sheave. The top slide had a mechanism that stopped the cutter at the rim of the sheave. The sheave was then turned round and the operation was repeated. Finally, using a hand-held chisel, the operator cut the rope groove in the rim. (Brewster *c*1811, plate LXI Fig 2, Science Museum/Science and Society Picture Library)

For efficient working, production rates of the individual components needed to match each other so that all came together for final assembly without having incurred any production bottlenecks. Brunel did note some production figures for individual machines in his notebook entitled 'Block Machinery',[15] but he does not give any indications as to the skills of the operators. Neither does he state 'whether they reflect a short-term trial under best conditions or are long-term run-of-the-mill averages that include the time required to change over the machine adjustments from one size block to another'.[16] Translating the timings quoted for some tasks into the necessary hand movements by the machine operators casts further doubt on these figures. Clearly, experience soon showed that there were some problems with obtaining matching production rates. In 1805 Brunel was seeking extra boring machines, and in 1806 Goodrich was seeking permission to purchase an additional engine for turning iron pins and two extra riveting engines, both to Brunel's designs and all to be manufactured by Maudslay.[17] Cooper's detailed analysis of the evidence led her to the broad conclusion that eventually 'the working rates of the machines were approximately matched and would permit a reasonably smooth flow of materials through the blockmill'.[18]

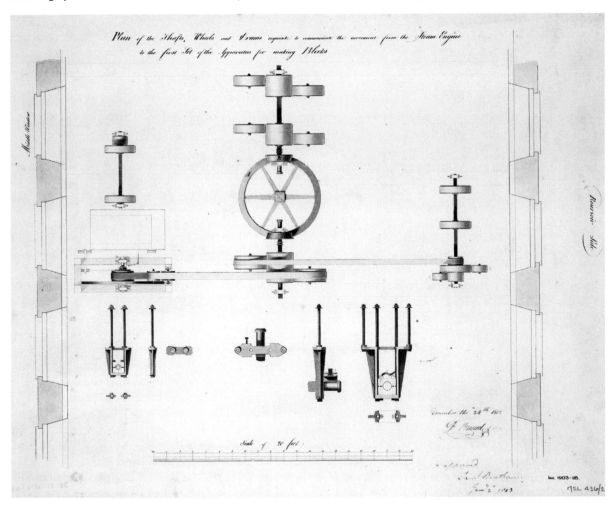

Figure 6.23 One of two (along with Fig 6.24) very early and rare drawings signed by Brunel on Christmas Eve 1802 and approved by Bentham on 2 January 1803. The arrangement is shown of part of the power transmission system in the south range, which must have then been nearing completion. (Science Museum/Science and Society Picture Library, MSL 436/2)

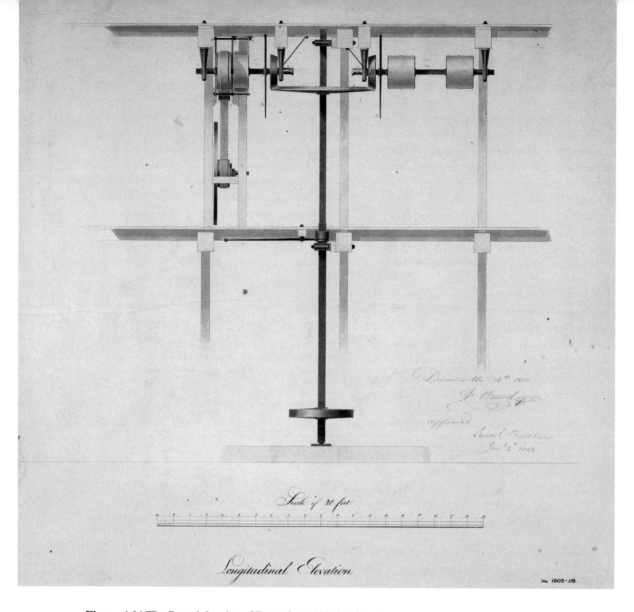

Longitudinal Elevation

Figure 6.24 The Brunel drawing of December 1802 showing the power transmission system proposed for the first floor of the south range. This is the only evidence to show that some of the block machinery was installed on this floor. This may have been a temporary arrangement pending completion of the rest of the ranges. (Science Museum/Science and Society Picture Library, MSL, 436/1)

For an idea of the original layout of the machines we are mainly dependent on the various articles in early encyclopaedias. However, a drawing signed by Brunel on 24 December 1802, and endorsed as 'approved' by Bentham on 2 January 1803, shows that the first set of block-making machinery was intended for installation on the first floor of the south range (Figs 6.23 and 6.24). This was probably a temporary measure, pending completion of the rest of the building and the arrival of the two further sets of machines.

By 1812 the first floor was apparently used as a storeroom and a workshop.[19] Another drawing of c1805 shows some of the overhead line shafts on the ground floor. Further archaeological evidence remains within the buildings themselves. Here, impressions of machinery bases, the wear occasioned by the operatives and bolt-holes in many of the floors indicate the locations of machines. These, however, require detailed examination and analysis, and some may well belong to more recent equipment.

The most helpful of the early articles is in Rees's *Cyclopaedia* (1812). This accurately describes the three main ranges of the buildings, noting that they contained other woodworking machinery in addition to the block-making machines. However, Rees seems to be on less sure ground when describing the actual location of individual machines. The southern range had its ground floor mostly occupied by the two steam engines, the boilers and the chain pumps. The upper part of the western beam engine also took up some of the space of the first floor, and the remainder was used as a storeroom and a workshop for small wooden articles. The second floor was a similar combination of storeroom and workshop; above this was the huge water tank that fed the dockyard mains and a series of pipes used for fire-fighting within the building itself. Rees lists a number of saws in the north range. On the ground floor he notes five circular and two reciprocating saws to convert elm for shells. On the first floor were three lignum vitae saws, 13 sheave-making machines, and five machines for turning and polishing pins. This list of saws does, however, differ significantly from those listed the previous year by Goodrich, who noted a

total of six saws, excluding the three cornering saws in the central range of the Block Mills. The second floor was largely given over to stores and workshops for small wooden articles. The preponderance of saws in this range led to its sometimes being referred to in the records as the sawmill.[20] In the single-storey central range were 14 shell-making machines, one large boring machine and two deadeye machines (Fig 6.25).

None of the encyclopaedias state the precise location of machines within these respective areas. The best evidence we have for a section of the early layout comes from a plan showing a part of the power-transmission system (see Appendix for a detailed description, and Endpapers for drawing). However, much remains unknown about the

Figure 6.25 The deadeye machine was a combination machine used for shaping the outside of the deadeye and for scoring the groove for the rope. Deadeyes were circular blocks that had no sheaves. Instead, their sides were pierced with three holes for lanyards. They were commonly used in pairs to secure the end of a shroud to a chain plate. After arriving from the corner-saw, the deadeye shell was fixed to the chuck by two adjustable pins that gripped two of the previously bored holes in the deadeye. In an operation very similar to that of the shaping machine, half the outside of the block was then shaped by the operator forcing a cutting tool against a curved former, simultaneously sweeping it across the deadeye. The operator then stopped the machine, slackened the chuck, reversed the deadeye and machined the other side. The outside of the deadeye was then scored using a slightly modified sequence of the system used on the scoring machines. The Block Mills had two deadeye machines, one for the smaller deadeyes from 4in to 10in (102–254mm), with a larger one for those from 11in to 19in (279–483mm). It was calculated that one man could shape and score about 11 7in (178mm) deadeyes an hour. (Rees's *Cyclopaedia*, 1812)

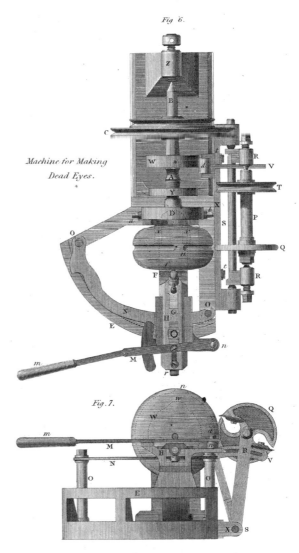

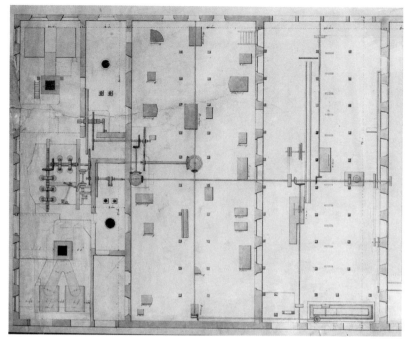

Figure 6.26 Part of an 1858 drawing of the ground floor of the Block Mills showing the engines, boiler rooms, pumps and the line shafting to the woodworking machinery. Compare the latter with Fig 6.27. (© National Maritime Museum, London, MS 184/149)

precise changes during the early years in the arrangement of the transmission systems within the building. From an early date all the machinery in the central range took its power from an overhead line shaft running the length of the range in the roof space (Figs 6.26 and 6.27). The line shafting that remains today matches a drawing of 1858; an undated but annotated drawing of around 1805 in the Goodrich Collection shows what may be the original similar overhead arrangement here.[21] Drums on this shaft are noted as driving various machines in the central range as well as the north range. Labels on these identify individual machines[22] and show that they were arranged in a hollow rectangle around the walls of the central range. Farey, writing in Rees's *Cyclopaedia*, perhaps unwittingly provides a clue as to the location of at least one of the shaping machines when he records an alarming accident. One of the wheels on the chuck cracked as the shaping machine was being operated. As a result, all 10 blocks flew off from the rear of the machine 'through the same pane of glass with great violence' and into one of the engine houses, where they smashed the engine governor.[23] This indicates that one at least of the shaping machines was located on the south side of the central range. This general layout lasted into the 20th century, as can be seen in the 1900 photograph (see Fig 4.6).

Although not a production line in the modern sense, this pioneering arrangement in this part of the Block Mills shows considerable logic. It positioned three sets of machines for each range of block sizes into small production groups around the sides of the room, reducing to a minimum the distance the processed material had to travel between machines (Fig 6.28). The least satisfactory part of the production sequence was at the very beginning, where the wood was first cut to size in the converting saws and then placed on the boring machines at the start of the three production groups. The more distant location of some of the converting saws and the widely spaced boring machines must have added to the volume of cross-floor and between-floor traffic. Indeed the latter must have made the two stairs in the buildings busy places (see Fig 4.8). Although Goodrich and Brunel were apparently considering an internal crane to help lessen this problem, there is no evidence that one was ever installed.[24]

There is no record of where the final assembly took place of the sheaves, pins and shells, or where the completed blocks were given their final polish. However, given both Bentham's and Brunel's keen desire to make the Block Mills a showcase for visitors, the likelihood is that these processes took place in the centre of the floor of the central range. This would allow visitors to stand at the

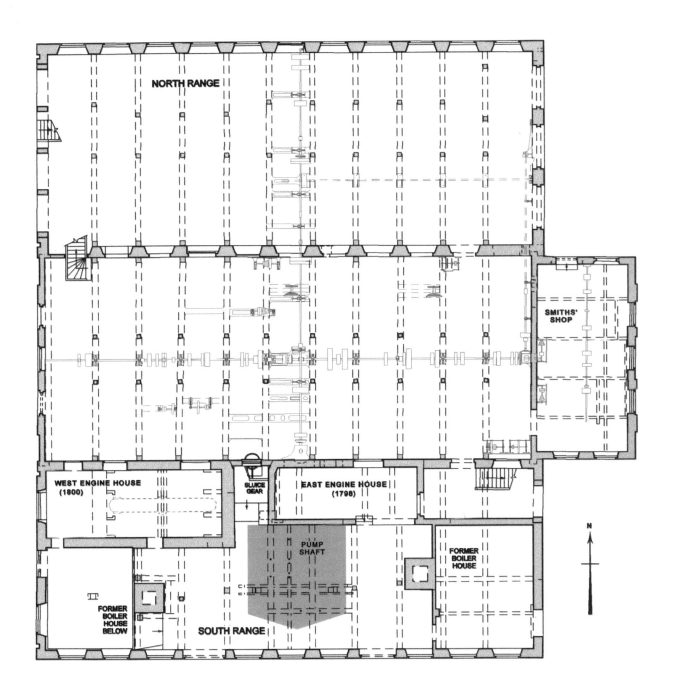

NORTH RANGE

SMITHS' SHOP

WEST ENGINE HOUSE (1800)

SLUICE GEAR

EAST ENGINE HOUSE (1798)

PUMP SHAFT

FORMER BOILER HOUSE

FORMER BOILER HOUSE BELOW

SOUTH RANGE

N

Figure 6.27 Ground-floor plan of the Block Mills showing the existing overhead line shafting, most of which dates from around the middle of the 19th century. (EH)

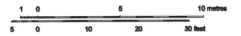

1   0   5   10 metres

5   0   10   20   30 feet

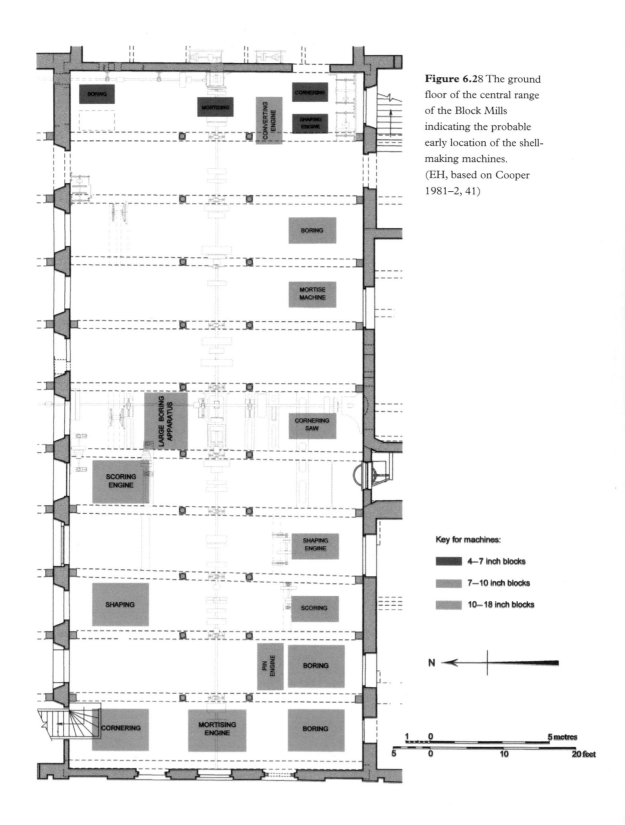

Figure 6.28 The ground floor of the central range of the Block Mills indicating the probable early location of the shell-making machines. (EH, based on Cooper 1981–2, 41)

BORING

MORTISING

CORNERING

CONVERTING ENGINE

SHAPING ENGINE

BORING

MORTISE MACHINE

LARGE BORING APPARATUS

CORNERING SAW

SCORING ENGINE

SHAPING ENGINE

SHAPING

SCORING

PIN ENGINE

BORING

CORNERING

MORTISING ENGINE

BORING

Key for machines:

4–7 inch blocks

7–10 inch blocks

10–18 inch blocks

N

1 0   5 metres

5 0   10   20 feet

western doorway and see the shell production – in many ways the most spectacular and complex part of the manufacturing process – going on in front of them as well as the final assembly of the blocks.

In 1808 the Block Mills came of age. The building was now responsible for the entire supply of blocks for the fleet. The 130,000 produced that year also gave Brunel and the Admiralty a basis on which to calculate the reward for his invention. At the start of the project it had been agreed that he would be paid a sum equal to the saving achieved in one year by the operation of his machinery compared to the previous production costs. The Admiralty's initial investment in the project was some £54,000.[25] Brunel calculated that on this basis he was due £21,174 12s 10d. In 1810, after protracted negotiations, the Admiralty paid him a total of £17,663 19s 0d.[26]

Savings in costs and concentration of production into one building did not, however, bring total peace of mind. In May 1806, even before the Block Mills had built up to their full production, Goodrich noted in his diary:

[Mr Brunel] had heard from some Gentlemen of the Admty that they think it necessary that there should be another establishment for Block making for fear that the Portsmouth establishment should be burnt down. Brunel shows me the sketch of a proposal he intends making his [sawmill] manufactory with machines capable of supplying all the Blocks used in the Navy in case of accident to the Portsmouth machinery.

Brunel also explained the financial arrangements he thought necessary if his idea was to proceed. Goodrich tartly noted in his diary: 'There appeared the usual veracity of a Frenchman in his statement.'[27] As nothing more is heard of this particular suggestion, it seems unlikely that Brunel installed such machinery. Ironically, it was his Battersea sawmills and not the Block Mills that caught fire and burnt down in 1814.

In 1815, no doubt spurred by the devastating effects of this fire, Brunel revived the idea of a duplicate set of block-making machines. This time, the Admiralty apparently took heed. Over the next two years, Brunel prepared a set of working drawings that incorporated a number of improvements and modifications gained in the light of experience at Portsmouth: 'the framings only of these machines . . . are cast and put together to be finished hereafter when thought proper, and that the forms and proportions of the framings in question have been made to correspond with the enlarged dimensions given to several of the machines.' Goodrich felt that if the machines were needed, Maudslay could fairly quickly manufacture the working parts.[28] The frames were apparently stored in one of the fireproof rooms in Brunel's new sawmills at Chatham Dockyard, where they were to remain in reserve.[29] What became of them is not known, but they may have been scrapped after a serious fire here in the mid-19th century.[30]

The fame of the block-making machinery has often obscured the other wood manufacturing processes that went on in the building. As early as May 1804 Goodrich listed some of the items produced on the sawing machinery here. Among these were oak hammock racks, oak tracing battens, grating battens, table legs and frames, ladders converted from oak boards, and cants cut out and rebated for bulkheads.[31] Slowly but gradually machinery was being applied to the manufacture of ships' fixtures and fittings. Some indication of the balance between functions of the Wood Mills and the Block Mills can be gauged from Bentham's February 1805 list of staff required for the former:[32]

1 master
30 wood millers
2 machine repairers
1 foreman of block-makers
20 block-makers 'including turners, house carpenters, or other artificers employed chiefly by making by hand such articles of blockmakers wares as it may not be advantageous to make by machinery'
2 sawyers
1 cabin keeper
8 labourers
10 boys
2 engine keepers.

Interestingly, despite this new machinery, the numbers of hand sawyers employed in Portsmouth continued to grow. In 1790 the yard employed 50 pairs; by 1811 this figure had risen to 95. Similarly, the numbers of house carpenters and joiners rose from 137 in 1790 to 404 in 1813.[33] Clearly, the demands of the Napoleonic Wars were the driving force in the same way that they spurred on the two mills. What we do not know is how far the output of the Wood Mills reduced the overall demand for sawyers, house carpenters and joiners.[34]

7 FAME

Both Bentham and Brunel were keenly aware of the benefits of publicity. This was not sought for egotistical reasons, although it would be rash to suggest these played no part. It was far more that both engineers were keen to bring to as wide an audience as possible the benefits of the new industrial processes and inventions. At Portsmouth they did not have long to wait.

Twelve days before Nelson visited the building in September 1805, Commissioner Saxton, with an entrepreneurial flair that his 21st-century successors might envy, 'started an idea about having a Box for strangers to pay into who wish to see the works, either at the Metal Mills or Woodmills'. Goodrich, who recorded this, clearly thought the Commissioner was rather mercenary. 'I told him I would consider about it but that it seemed a thing that required some consideration'.[1] Nothing more was heard of this proposal.

Saxton's suggestion may have been prompted by a desire to reduce the numbers making their way to the building. Even in wartime Georgian England, visitors wishing to see inside the royal dockyards needed little more than an introduction from a local hotelier or a prominent local citizen. In May 1805 Brunel had noted in his journal that 'this frequent admission of visitors is of great hindrance to the men at work'. On 1 July he noted 'The place was the whole morning crowded with visitors, much to the annoyance of the service.'[2] On 12 July, Brunel visited Bentham and asked if he would permit the Wood Mills to be surrounded by a fence to prevent intruders. Nothing was done. In desperation, Brunel wrote to the commissioner that 'the works carried on at the wood-mill are considerably impeded by the number of persons who are daily admitted to the place. No regularity can be obtained when the shops are crowded with strangers. The men cannot be overlooked and kept in that state of activity so requisite in a manufactory.'[3] It seems that some sort of control of visitors to the Block Mills must have been introduced soon afterwards, for the complaints about the crowds largely cease.

Nevertheless, the buildings remained a magnet for the curious. A substantial proportion of those visitors whose names do appear in the records were, as might be expected, senior members of the Admiralty or Navy Boards. Less welcome were delegations on official inspections. Goodrich gloomily noted in his diary at the end of January 1807:

as ill luck seldom comes alone it happens now that the Metal Mills are standing owing to the crank gudgeon

having worked loose, there are five gentlemen arrived at Portsmouth to take a survey of the works of the dockyard. Viz Mr Rennie, Mr Watts jr, Mr Southern [Watt's partner], Mr Whidby from Woolwich and the Secretary from the Board of Revision.[4]

By the time they left three days later, Goodrich had developed a strong dislike of Rennie, noting in his diary that 'his observations convince me that he is deficient in experience and judgement about such matters [the main dock pumps] or that he willingly slanders'.[5] In July 1810 Goodrich took the Persian ambassador round the Block Mills. More fun perhaps was his October guided tour taking 'Miss Fox and others of Ld Holland's connections'.[6]

At the end of 1812 the posts of inspector general of naval works and those of his staff were abolished. For a while Simon Goodrich found only short-term contract employment with the navy, but the latter could ill afford the loss of his skills. On 2 March 1814 he was formally appointed as engineer and mechanist. He was to be based at Portsmouth, as he noted with some pride in his diary, 'upon the same salary and footing as Mr Holl'.[7] The appointment, as well as giving him an annual income of £600, allowed him a draughtsman and a clerk. At the same time, the masters of the Wood Mills and the Metal Mills and the millwrights were given salaries of £250, and each was allowed a foreman and a cabin keeper.[8] In these appointments are the seeds of the mechanical engineering and production departments in the royal dockyards.

On 18 June, Goodrich arrived at Portsmouth on the mail coach with his wife and family, just in time to play a part in the great allied celebrations following the Treaty of Paris. On 24 June the royal party headed by the Prince Regent, with the Emperor of Russia, the King of Prussia, Marshall Blucher and others, inspected the fleet and visited the dockyard. In a brief entry in his diary, Goodrich wrote: 'At Dockyard, Portsmouth. Attend at Wood Mills and Metal Mills upon the great folk.'[9] Goodrich rarely let his personal feelings intrude into his writings, but this terse entry may well have been occasioned by the presence of Samuel Bentham, who no doubt stole some of his glory. However, as a bonus, we do have a more lively account of this visit written by 14-year-old George Bentham, Samuel's son:

My father ... though no longer in Office, was privileged as being the chief author of the most important establishments in the Yard, and was officially present among those who attended upon the Sovereigns, had taken my brother, myself and Philip Abbot in the day before – we spent the night in the Office of the Master of the Wood Mills, and awaited in those Mills the Imperial and Royal Party. Alexander, on learning who we were, said some very civil things to us to our great gratification.[10]

For a 14-year-old boy, the excitement of a night in the Block Mills followed by meeting the royal party and their entourage there the next day understandably made a deep impression. His father would no doubt have been even more gratified to read the account of the visit in The Times (Fig 7.1). The paper noted that two days were devoted to looking at warships and the dockyard: 'But the Emperor and the King appeared more peculiarly interested by that unequalled system of machinery for making the ships' blocks, the rapid operations of which they witnessed with particular pleasure. All expressed their admiration of the mechanism, which they thought was of itself well worth coming to Portsmouth to see.'[11]

Once the Block Mills began to feature in various encyclopaedias, their fame quickly grew. Visits were not confined to politicians, the military and men of science. In June 1822 the novelist Maria Edgeworth, by then in her fifties, wrote to her stepmother:

We have accomplished, much to our satisfaction, our long intended journey to Portsmouth ... Lady Grey, wife of the Commissioner, ordered all works in the dockyard to be opened to us ... And now for the Block Machinery you will say, but it is impossible to describe this in a letter of moderate or immoderate size. I will only say that the ingenuity and successful performance far surpassed my expectations. Machinery so perfect appears to act with the happy certainty of instinct and the foresight of reason combined.[12]

This certainly conveys Maria's enthusiasm for what she saw, but it may be doubted that her stepmother was any the wiser from this description.

Well into the nineteenth century, the Block Mills remained a seemingly unlikely tourist attraction that apparently appealed not only to both sexes but also to all ages. In 1831 Sir Walter Scott took his daughters to Portsmouth Dockyard and noted in his diary: 'The girls break loose, mad with the craze of seeing sights ... The girls contrive to secure sight of the Block Manufactory ... I think I have seen these wonderful sights in 1816 or about

that time.'[13] The previous October the Duchess of Kent and the 11-year-old Princess Victoria had visited the dockyard. There is no record of the young princess breaking loose 'mad with delight'. However, the ever-faithful Goodrich was on hand to show her and her mother round the Block Mills, 'and I explain the machinery of the Wood Mills to them. This is my birthday.'[14]

Perhaps inevitably, as memories dimmed and those directly responsible for the creation of the original machinery died, some controversy developed over the precise contributions of Brunel and Bentham to the block-making machinery. Professor Robert Willis noted in a lecture delivered to the Society of Arts in 1851 that 'the whole of the machinery in Portsmouth Dockyard has usually been popularly ascribed to Brunel alone'.[15] The following year the widowed Lady Bentham published a comprehensive paper in answer to this. In it she noted that, though Brunel was entirely responsible for the machinery for the shaping and finishing of the blocks, the preliminary preparation of the timber blanks was done on Bentham-designed saws. Moreover, the actual layout of the machinery was the responsibility of Bentham's staff.[16] Simon Goodrich, who nearly half a century earlier had been directly responsible for setting up the Wood Mills and for installing the block-making machinery, and whose contemporary correspondence with the Admiralty essentially corroborated Lady Bentham's account, had died five years earlier in Portugal. Had he still been alive, he would no doubt have rallied to the defence of his old chief. This might have stopped Beamish in 1862 from dismissing Lady Bentham's claims in his biography of Marc Brunel and muddying the waters further by erroneously asserting that she was claiming that her husband had invented all the machinery.[17]

Although the mid-century controversy over who should be credited for the various machines stirred passions, it did not diminish the popularity of the Block Mills. For much of the 19th century they remained one of the great attractions of Portsmouth, the numerous encyclopaedia articles bringing the fame of the machinery to a wide audience.[18] As the century wore on, other industrial marvels gradually captured the public imagination. By the time the Institution of Mechanical Engineers held their meeting in Portsmouth in July 1892, the Block Mills were becoming something of an antiquarian curiosity. Their fame as the pioneering factory using machine tools for mass production was assured, but by then the need for blocks was decreasing sharply as steam replaced sail.

IMPERIAL & ROYAL VISIT to PORTSMOUTH.

Portsmouth, Saturday morning, eight o'clock.

The Dock-yard, yesterday morning, engaged the attention of our illustrious visitors. The Prince Regent, the Duke of York (with much military splendour), and the King of Prussia, the Prussian Princes, the other Princes of Germany, and a large assemblage of distinguished individuals, native and foreign, repaired early to the Emperor Alexander, at Commissioner Grey's house, whence they proceeded to view the various establishments. The ships building or repairing in the slips, the immense naval stores of every description in the warehouses, the rope-house, the copper-works, and all the other important branches, were examined with much attention. But the Emperor and the King appeared more peculiarly interested by that unequalled system of machinery for making the ships' blocks, the rapid operations of which they witnessed with particular pleasure. All expressed their admiration of the mechanism, which they thought was of itself well worth coming to Portsmouth to see. The numerous objects of curiosity and utility in the yard occupied all the forenoon.

About two o'clock the royal barges, with the whole party, and the rest of the grand aquatic procession, left the King's Stairs at the Dock Yard in the same order as the day before, to pay another and a longer visit to the fleet in the Roads. Royal salutes were fired from all the batteries. On their arrival at the fleet, the Prince Regent, King and Princes of Prussia, and many others, went on board the Royal Sovereign yacht, which immediately hoisted the Royal Standard. The Emperor Alexander had previously gone with the Duke of Clarence on board the Impregnable, the interior of which seems to afford his Imperial Majesty peculiar delight. He was as assiduous as before, in making himself personally acquainted with nautical arrangements. The fleet, consisting of 15 sail of the line, and about the same number of frigates, formed a line of seven or eight miles in extent, in front of the Isle of Wight. They received the Royal Visitors with a general salute, after which they slipped their cables, and were immediately under sail with a brisk north-east gale. They speedily cleared St. Helen's, and went quite out to sea, The Royal Sovereign yacht led the van. The yachts and barges of the Admiralty, the Naval Commissioners, the Ordnance, and other public offices, a great number of private yachts, and above 200 vessels of all descriptions, sailed out, keeping at various distances from the fleet. About five o'clock the whole line-of-battle ships hove to by signal, when the Prince Regent, the King of Prussia, the Prussian and other Princes, left the Royal Sovereign, and went to the Emperor of Russia and his party in the Impregnable, to which the Royal Standard was accordingly shifted. At this time the leading ships were about 12 miles from Portsmouth. The Royal circle partook of some entertainment in the Impregnable's cabin. The signal was made soon afterwards for the return of all the ships of war to their anchorage, where they were reviewed on Thursday. The wind was not so favourable for sailing back ; but the general effect of so many vessels of war and pleasure-boats, turning to windward through a narrow channel, the men of war ranging up alongside the smaller vessels, and the frequent repetition of signals in both directions along the line, together with the amazing accuracy of the naval movements, was of the most beautiful and of the grandest kind imaginable. As they returned, they continued their firing, so as to afford, in some respects, the idea of a naval engagement. In the visit of Thursday the ships lay at anchor, with their sails down ; in that of yesterday they displayed, before assembled Sovereigns, the proudest boast of this sea-girt isle—a British fleet in a state of activity. In the course of the night and morning, many private vessels had come in from various parts of the coast, so that the number had considerably increased since Thursday. The day was certainly more like one in October than in June, but it was not forbidding. Gleams of solar glory occasionally elicited the green of the ocean, or lighted to view the undulating beauties and umbrageous richness of the Isle of Wight ; or set forth, with all

George Inn, in front of which sentinels have been placed. The whole town is again illuminated, and with additional splendour. The Duke of Wellington's initials are on the George Inn.

Saturday Evening.

His Grace the Duke of Wellington left us early this morning for London. The last grand spectacle was that of the military in review order on Portsdown-hill. At eleven o'clock the Prince Regent, and the Allied Sovereigns and retinue, left Portsmouth for Portsdown-hill. About 7,000 troops were drawn up in review order, and the Regent and the illustrious Visitors having stationed themselves in front of the line on horseback, the infantry passed by in companies in review order, the dragoons keeping the ground. The Prince Regent rode his beautiful white charger, and the Allied Potentates, the Generals, and suite, were mounted likewise. The line was then formed, and the Prince Regent and their Majesties rode down and inspected them, and then drove off for Goodwood, to breakfast with the Duke of Richmond. From thence the Royal party will proceed to Petworth, the seat of the Earl of Egremont, to dine and sleep, and afterwards to Brighton.— Thus has ended the grandest scene perhaps ever witnessed in this or any other country.

The Prince Regent will take farewell of his distinguished visitors at the Pavillion, at Brighton, on Monday ; from which town the Regent returns to Carlton-house. The Emperor of Russia, on his arrival at Dover, will embark in the Magicienne, for Helvoetsluys. The Duke of Clarence shifted his flag this evening to that ship. The King of Prussia will embark in the Jason, for Calais, which ship will bear the flag of Rear Admiral Blackwood. The Nymphen, Capt. M. Smith, will take across the gallant Generals, &c. to whatever port they may desire to be landed at.

The military and the populace have behaved extremely orderly and well.

The Prince Regent, after the Levee this morning, presented the Honourable George Grey, Commissioner of this Dock-yard, with the patent of a Baronetcy ; and conferred the honour of Knighthood on the following Officers. Vice-Admiral George Martin ; Henry White, Esq. Mayor of this Borough ; Capt. Freeman Barton, of the 2d or Queen's regiment ; Colonel Robarts, of the 10th Hussars : the two latter Officers commanded the Guards of Honour on this visit. Admirals Sir Edmund Nagle, and Sir John Poo Beresford, kissed hands on being appointed Naval Aides-de-Camp to the Regent ; as did also Colonels Barnard, Craven, and Harvey, on being appointed Aides-de-Camp. General Bailey was the Equerry in waiting, and Lord Forbes Aide-de-Camp in waiting, during the visit.

It has been long a custom, on the first visit of the ruler of the nation to this Royal Dock-yard, to give to the artificers and labourers a week's pay, called by them the "King's Bounty." This favour was among the Regent's bestowments this day, and, with it, an half holyday.

During the review of the fleet at Spithead, on Thursday, the King of Prussia was struck with the appearance of a barge of the Rodney, ship rigged, sailing about the fleet, and requested her as a present of the Prince Regent. His Royal Highness immediately consented with his usual condescension ; when the King, turning round to the Regent and the Emperor, facetiously observed, "I hope you two heads of great maritime nations will not be jealous of my Navy."

The Regent, on taking his departure from

Figure 7.1 Extract from *The Times* of 27 June 1814 of the allied sovereigns' visit to Portsmouth and their view of the Block Mills. (By permission of the Syndics of Cambridge University Library)

8 THE LATER YEARS

Once the Wood Mills had been completed and the various machines had been installed and were operating satisfactorily, references to them become far less frequent in the official records. In 1815 the original chimneys were causing problems. The heat of the boiler furnaces had caused the chimneys to crack. As Goodrich noted, 'as these chimneys pass through the building, and are surrounded with a casing of wood in the floors above, there might be some danger of fire'.[1] His own preference was to make the 'upper part of the shaft round, to lessen the eddy of the wind' and to increase the overall height by some 10ft (3m). It had been found by experience that the wind eddies tended to drive the smoke down onto the large open water tanks that formed the roofs of both the main ranges, causing 'the smoke to beat down very much upon the water . . . and to descend too much upon the other buildings'.[2] It seems that both chimneys were rebuilt the following year.

By 1830 the Murray and Wood table engine was showing signs of wear and was replaced by a Maudslay beam engine installed in the same location. Given the limited space and headroom of the original Sadler engine house, this operation seems to have involved lowering the floor. Seven years later the original Boulton and Watt engine likewise was replaced by a new one from the same manufacturer. Parts of this engine remain in position in the west engine house (Figs 8.1, 8.2 and 8.3). These two new beam engines apparently continued to supply the motive power to the line shafts until replaced by electric motors in 1911.

The increasing number of steam-driven machines in the royal dockyards, the gradual introduction in the late 1820s of steam propulsion into naval vessels and the general national shortage of skilled engineers was forcing the navy to begin training its own. In April 1831 Thomas Lloyd was

Figure 8.1 Part of the frame of the 1837 Boulton and Watt engine in the western engine house in the south range. A photograph taken in 2003. (EH, AA 042388)

Figure 8.2 Looking north-east across the Great Basin to the Block Mills (photograph taken in October 1897). The Block Mills lies just to the left of Docks 3, 4 and 5, each covered by timber roofs. Dominating the Block Mills on its left is the huge smithery built between 1852 and 1855 to a design by G T Greene. This rare photograph shows the Block Mills still with its two boiler chimneys. (© National Maritime Museum, London, N11569)

appointed as superintendent of the Block Mills. Between 1819 and 1826 he had studied at the nearby School of Naval Architecture and had been recommended for the Block Mills post by Professor Inman, best known for his nautical tables. Lloyd was clearly an able man; less than two years later he was appointed to be inspector of machinery at Woolwich.[3]

The middle of the 19th century also saw a major expansion of the woodworking capacity in the dockyard.

A complete new sawmill was built in 1848 as part of the new Steam Factory complex adjacent to the Steam Basin.[4] Probably a few years before then, a substantial single-storey range was built onto the northern side of the north range of the Wood Mills (Fig 8.4). This was described as a vertical sawmill, its plan showing it incorporating a narrow grindstone house on its southern side. On the north side a new engine and boiler house were constructed to power the machinery. Apart from an early plan and elevation drawing,[5] little is known about this extension, which was demolished some years before the First World War. Only its scar remains.

Retrenchments in the Royal Navy in the years following the ending of the Napoleonic Wars would have meant a reduction from the wartime peak need for blocks. But the peacetime demands of a fleet that remained active exercising the *Pax Britannica*, protecting the trade routes of empire, dealing with the Barbary corsairs and mounting the anti-slavery patrols ensured a steady demand for the products of the Block Mills. It did not, however, save the Block Mills from the retrenchments, reforms and staff cuts introduced in the early 1830s by the First Lord of the Admiralty Sir James Graham. By 1838 the Block Mills were the responsibility of Robert Taplin, an engineer trained by Goodrich. In addition to the Block Mills, Taplin was responsible for all the yard machinery, the work in the new boiler house and the operation of the Metal Mills.[6]

An 1854 printed list of products manufactured at the Block Mills has blocks ranging in size from 4in (102mm) to 'above 24 inches'. Each size of block was available as a single, double, treble, topsail sheet, clew-line, long tackle, sister, ninepin, deadeye and heart. The factory also produced planked or built block-shells for careening and other purposes. The shells for these were made by hand. The final part of the manufacturing process for all the

Figure 8.3 First floor of the south range, looking west. This clearly shows the east wall of the 1800 Boulton and Watt engine house encapsulated within the slightly later south range of the Wood Mills. (EH, AA 042419)

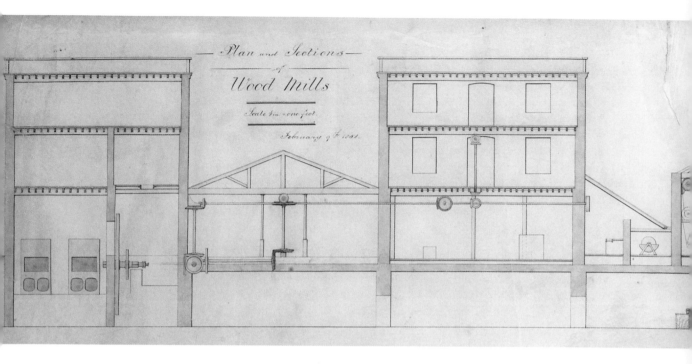

Figure 8.4 A cross-section of the Wood Mills in 1858 showing the location of the line shafting. To the left two boilers are shown. On the right is a lean-to extension that was used as a grindstone house; beyond this to the north were built the vertical sawmills. Both of the latter were subsequently demolished. (© National Maritime Museum, London, MS 184/149)

blocks was 'to mark with the broad arrow in four places, and with the number of the month and year in which the block shells and sheaves are made'.[7]

This same source also lists the wide range of items manufactured by the Wood Mills. As might be expected, most of these were fittings for warships. Among these were capstans of all sizes; compass stands; handles for pumps, bells and winches; cups 'for pay tables'; pump boxes; 'racks: shot, arms'; steering wheels 'for ships of the line'; tables, 'hanging, circular'; and 'tubs – boats'. Drawers, handles and knobs were also produced for the house carpenters and shipwrights fitting out the galley areas and the officers' cabins in warships. Rollers were produced for boats' stages as well as for window blinds. For dockyard craftsmen, the Wood Mills manufactured some of the parts of the tools of their trade – astragals, helves, mallets and mandrels are listed. Similarly, the dockyard police force were supplied with 'Batons for Constables'. Pins for bayonets also appear in the list: presumably these were metal and manufactured as offshoots of the pins required

for the coaks of the blocks. Among the more unusual items were squeegees and office rulers – the latter probably manufactured and engraved mechanically.[8]

This list, however, does not do justice to the larger items processed in the building as are evidenced by the survival of a number of substantial machines that are not connected with block-making. In 1853 the Block Mills took delivery of a massive horizontal wood boring machine that was capable of boring a 4ft (1.2m) diameter hole to a depth of 3ft (0.9m). Equally massive was an overhead plane – a trying-up machine – installed in 1890 and in use until 1970. It is still in the building. This huge machine could plane a baulk of timber 24in (610mm) wide, 17in (432mm) thick and up to 15ft (4.6m) long. In later years it processed large sections of timber for HMS *Victory* and prepared dock blocks.[9]

Unfortunately, no annual production figures survive. Although a certain number of the smaller and more standard items may have been kept in stock, most were probably manufactured on demand. Similarly, the strength of the labour force employed here at that time is not known. However, a manuscript book recording the names and addresses of the Wood Mill employees does survive for the years c1864 to c1902. This source would seem to indicate that in the period 1860–80 around 50 people were employed in the Block Mills, with a further 27 working in the sawmills.[10] This last figure presumably includes those working in the new extension added some years before.

By the middle of the 19th century the Royal Navy's warships were starting to change. By then, ships of the line were being fitted with steam engines, although these were seen only as auxiliary providers of power, principally for manoeuvring in and out of harbour. The fleet remained fully rigged, and sails remained supreme. In consequence, the products of the Block Mills continued in substantial and regular demand. Even the launch of HMS *Warrior* in 1860 was probably not perceived by the block-makers as posing any threat to their livelihood. HMS *Warrior's* hull was revolutionary – the first all-metal armour-plated warship in the world – but she remained a full-rigged ship and for most purposes was expected to use her sails rather than her engines. Her main armament of shell guns was also new and vastly more powerful than the smooth-bore guns that had evolved with the fleet since the time of the early Tudors. However, although fewer in number than the smooth bore weapons carried on the largest ships of the line, the new shell guns were still mounted as broadside weapons, and early designs still required blocks and tackle to manoeuvre them and breeching ropes to restrain the recoil. HMS *Warrior* inaugurated a revolution for the Royal Navy's capital ships. Initially, she and her sister ships – collectively known as the Black Battlefleet on account of their hull colour – may well have provided increased work for the Portsmouth block-makers. The sheer size of these iron warships enabled them to carry vast acreages of canvas. *Agincourt*, *Minotaur* and *Northumberland* were each fitted with five masts, more than any other Royal Navy ship.[11] Inevitably, this led to a correspondingly huge requirement for standing and running rigging with all the blocks necessary to operate the yards and sails.

Experience, however, soon showed that these great ironclads on the whole were very poor sailers, while their lack of manoeuvrability under canvas made close fleet evolutions hazardous, if not impossible.[12] But the 1860s were to usher in the age of accelerating obsolescence for the Royal Navy, as new technical developments followed in swift succession. Marine steam engines gained in power, reliability and economy. Guns grew in range, size and accuracy. In 1870 HMS *Devastation* combined these two strands by becoming the Royal Navy's first capital ship to rely wholly on steam power, to dispense entirely with rigging and sails, and to mount her main armament fore and aft in turrets. Her turret guns were mechanically trained and required no blocks and tackle. Use of blocks on her pole masts was virtually confined to signal halyards. Elsewhere on board, she needed a small number of blocks for the derricks used for hoisting her ship's boats and for various purposes. Overall, her requirement for blocks was tiny compared to that of HMS *Victory*.

But sail did not give up without a fight. For imperial policing purposes in the quieter and remoter backwaters of empire, small sailing warships, with auxiliary engines, were ideal. Wind as motive power was free and limitless, if not always reliable. Even the most economical steam engines needed large quantities of coal that had to be expensively stockpiled in coaling stations. Although fully rigged warships had almost vanished from the main fleet by the late 1880s, smaller sailing warships continued to be built into the 20th century. The last to be constructed were 16 steel sloops launched between 1891 and 1903.[13] But well before then, demand for blocks had been declining rapidly. At Portsmouth a pointer to the future, with its reduced needs for rigging, had been the closing of the great ropery in 1868.[14]

In the 50 years before 1900, Portsmouth Dockyard had reinvented itself, expanding up harbour and constructing a vast industrial enterprise geared to building and servicing the new metal-hulled, steam-driven navy. Foundries, machine shops, armour-plate workshops, basins and docks were built on a scale that was vastly greater than their Georgian predecessors. Boiler chimneys dotted the skyline, railway lines snaked round the dockyard, huge heaps of coal bore dusty witness to the power of steam afloat and ashore.[15] The Block Mills were gradually subsumed, their chimneys no longer the focal points they had once been (Fig 8.5). In 1906 the first electricity generating station was completed in Portsmouth Dockyard, and in 1911 the steam engines at the Block Mills were replaced by electric motors, although most of the machines still obtained their power via the overhead shafting.[16] The beam engines were largely dismantled, although some of the 1837 Boulton and Watt engine remains in position. The boilers were removed and the chimneys were demolished to just below the roof level of the south range.[17]

Figure 8.5 Looking west over the northern end of Portsmouth Dockyard at the end of the 19th century. The Block Mills lie just to the right of the top of the tall chimney on the left. The contrast in scale between Georgian and Victorian technology is very apparent. (J G Coad)

The Block Mills nevertheless remained in use well into the 20th century, their products still in demand for some of the internal fittings of warships. Block-making also continued, although on a much reduced scale (Fig 8.6). Some of the processes involved in block-manufacturing gradually changed. By 1900 the Brunel pin-polishing machines were already out of use and considered obsolete. As demand for blocks further declined, it is likely that these and other block-making machines were taken out of production, and most were scrapped. The pin-turning lathe may well have been phased out as early as the 1830s, since engineers' screw-cutting lathes capable of making a smooth finish to the metal were readily available and used in many workshops. In the twentieth century the historic value of the Brunel machinery was clearly recognised by the Admiralty, and between 1933 and 1951

a representative group of eight machines was acquired by the Science Museum.

The last block-maker apprentice was entered in 1945, and nine years later the block-maker craft was absorbed into that of the shipwright. By the early 1960s annual production had fallen to around 2,000 blocks, the great majority made of metal and manufactured and repaired in the Shipwrights' Shop. These were produced by seven block-makers, one machinist and a part-time supervisor. In 1964 a further three machines were transferred to Portsmouth City Museum. In 1965 production of blocks in the Block Mills on the Brunel machines finally came to an end. The remaining workers and some of the machinery were redeployed to No. 6 Boathouse, where limited block-making continued until the beginning of 1983, although it was hampered in later years by the lack of suitable timber following the ravages of Dutch elm disease.[18] The only remaining occupants of the Block Mills were a group of hose-makers on the upper floors of the south range who remained there into the early 1980s. Fittingly, in 1965 the Science Museum published its monograph on the Block Mills, the first modern work on the subject.[19] In 1966 official recognition of the importance of the building and its surviving *in situ* machinery led to its being scheduled as an ancient monument.

Although its significance has been appreciated by many, the building has remained largely disused and empty since the early 1980s. In 2003 English Heritage carried out a detailed survey of the structure that has shed considerable light on the evolution of the Block Mills as a building.[20] More, however, remains to be learnt from a detailed study of the archaeological evidence of the marks and fixing points of machinery throughout the building. If this is done, it may prove possible to shed more light on the location of the Brunel and Bentham machinery.[21] However, enough is already known about the Block Mills to place it firmly in the category of one of the most significant industrial buildings to survive anywhere.

Figure 8.6 The Block Mills early in the 20th century, the north range still with its parapets and roof intact. (J G Coad)

APPENDIX

Machine drives: power transmission

Tony Woolrich

The sequence of the changes in the layout of the transmission gear is hard to resolve from the documentation so far discovered. The only early drawing showing any drives is dated after 1800 and relates to the installation of the Boulton and Watt engine.[1] This also shows the Sadler engine and the upper plan of the chain pumps and their gearing. The two steam engines were to be geared together so that transmission shafts came off both sides of the engine houses. The engines could be used independently or together by altering the gearing. One set of shafts drove the chain pumps, the salt-water reciprocating pump, and the reciprocating shaft in the tunnel which drove the freshwater pump in the deep well south-east of the building. The other drive shaft served the middle and north ranges and appears to have been designed to have been located in the vaults as an underdrive. This drawing possibly pre-dates the construction of the vaults, the north range and the roofing of the space between the ranges to house Brunel's block machines.

The drawing Goodrich prepared for the replacement to the Sadler engine in 1807 shows that the line of the shaft across the area of the vault had altered. The position of the cylinder in the engine house was the reverse of the position of the Sadler engine. This drawing also shows the centre lines of the drive shafts to be some 4ft (1.2m) below the floor line of the south range.[2]

A bill in the Goodrich Collection dated 10 January 1803 lists the components supplied for the millwright. The total cost was £774 6s 7d.[3] This lists gears of 9ft, 6ft, 5ft 4in and 3ft 4in (2.74, 1.83, 1.63 and 1.02m) in diameter, various cast-iron shafts and plummer-blocks, and numerous other components. Without detailed drawings or written notes it is impossible to interpret this with any more certainty, but it is clear this relates to the provision of the transmission gear. Some may relate to the drives for the chain pumps, but there are no parts of the chain pumps themselves included.

The undated drawing in the Goodrich Collection[4] shows an elevation of the whole of the overhead power transmission system in the central range, and part of the information drawn on it was added subsequent to the initial drawing (see Endpapers). The shaft had on it a number of long drums from which belts or ropes passed to intermediate pulleys (or riggers) located just under the roof at the sides of the middle range. More ropes or belts drove downward to the machines from these pulleys. A horizontal gear and two bevel gears are shown, indicating that the two halves of the shaft rotated in opposite directions. The vertical shaft for this gear is on the same centre-line as the shaft driven by the two steam engines noted above.

Most of the pulleys on this drawing are noted as driving machines in the central range, but one pulley drove a saw in the southern range and others drove drums in the northern range, presumably on another line shaft. This implies that at that stage there was no direct drive shaft from the engines to the northern range, and the machines there were driven from these drums. Dr Cooper used this drawing to work out the positioning of the machines in the middle range, but she discounted this information when making her evaluation.[5] The fact that there were no underdrives at the time this drawing was made is backed up by drawings made in 1803 of Bentham's saws, and the account of the horizontal cross-cutting saw in Rees's *Cyclopaedia*. In these, both of the drive shafts were suspended from the ceiling above. It is clear that underdrives were introduced soon after this, but the precise details have not yet been found. A drawing in the Goodrich Collection[6] shows the drive to the capstan from a shaft in the ceiling.

The Goodrich Collection has a much later letter, dated 11 August 1829, about the supply of parts to the millwright. These comprised a cast-iron shaft 13ft 2in (4.01m) long; two cast-iron bevel wheels, one 5ft 6in (1.68m) and the other 2ft 9in (838mm) in diameter; and two mitre wheels 1ft 7$\frac{1}{2}$in (495mm) in diameter. These wheel diameters accord with the gears noted on the 1807 Goodrich drawing above, so may relate to replacements.

The National Maritime Museum has a drawing dated 1858[7] showing the layout of the replacement steam engines, and machines and the line shafting to drive them, which accord with the remains of the drives as they are today (see Figs 6.26 and 8.4). This drawing shows the drives were split, although there was a geared link between the two engines, probably to be used if one or the other was out of action. The Boulton and Watt engine drove the shaft in the roof space the length of the centre range. From that, a shaft transmitted power along the west wall of the centre range into the north building, then a vertical shaft linked a longitudinal shaft on the first floor of the north range.

The Maudslay engine drove the chain pumps, and horizontal spear drive to the deep well and the salt-water pump. With the exception of the deep well, these were all in the south range. It also drove a shaft across the roof of the centre building, from which no machinery appears to have been driven, into the ground floor of the north building, where it drove various saws, and into the later lean-to annexe, where it drove grindstones. The sawing machines in the later building beyond that annexe were powered by an independent steam engine.

Drive details

The long drive drums on the shaft shown on the endpapers were undoubtedly built up from wooden staves and circular end pieces like straight-sided barrels. The drives from these would have been by endless flat leather belts perhaps to narrow cast-iron pulleys on intermediate shafts. This drawing also shows grooved pulleys, clearly intended for endless spliced ropes. The surviving drives today show mostly thin-wall solid cast-iron pulleys, which were threaded over the shafts and staked into place by four keys. This meant that once fixed it was hard to move the positions of the machines underneath. A few survive where the pulley and spokes have been smashed off, leaving just the centre boss and keys, for they were probably too hard to remove. There are a few split-pressed sheet-metal pulleys, added later in the 19th century, which could be positioned by clasping them around the shaft and tightening bolts. The shafts were supported by bearings held by hangers spaced out along the lengths of the buildings and bolted to the overhead timbers. They were lubricated by oil bottles inverted over the top bearing caps.

A number of sets of overhead countershafts and striking gear survive in the middle range, with very elegant standards. They undoubtedly date from Maudslay's time. There are a number of built-up wooden grooved pulleys for rope drives as well. Their age is unknown, but with all the woodworkers the dockyard employed, they were perhaps cheaper to make in this way than to buy metal ones.

NOTES

The following abbreviations have been used here

EH	English Heritage
GC	Goodrich Collection
NA	National Archives
NMM	National Maritime Museum
SML	Science Museum Library
UC	University College, London

Foreword

1   Partington, 1835.

Prologue

1   Oman 1968, 525.
2   McGowan 1999, 21.
3   Morriss 1983, 154.
4   NA, Progress Books, ADM 180/10 and 11.
5   GC, Book 10, 14.9.1805.

Chapter 1

1   Accurate calculations of the number of naval vessels at any given time depends to an extent on the definition of a naval ship. These figures come from Archibald 1972, 132–52. It should be noted that the 1805 total includes 175 ships of the line at one end, and 125 gun vessels and 62 hoys, lighters and transports at the other. The wartime strength of the Royal Navy was to peak a few years later. For a more conservative and detailed estimate that concentrates on the fighting vessels, see Rodgers (2004) 606–17.
2   Coad 1989, 1–3; Raddall 1993, 54; Raymond 1999, 2.
3   Rodger 1986, 29.
4   Coad 1981, 19–21.
5   Coad 1989, 26.
6   Archibald 1972, 44, 128; Coad 1989, 15.
7   McGowan 1999, 90.
8   Coad 1983, 352; Coad 1989, 94.
9   NA, ADM 140/555, parts 2–16; Coad 1989, 101–7.
10   Coad 1989, 23.
11   Skempton 2002, xvii.
12   Morriss 1983: chapter 6 gives an excellent account of dockyard management at this time.
13   Burton 1975, 71–7.
14   Dickinson 1939, 31–2, 61–3, 82–3.
15   Ibid, 83.
16   Patent No. 1552.
17   I am grateful to Tony Woolrich for drawing my attention to these examples.
18   Skempton 2002, 28–9; Skempton and Johnson 1962, 25–7.
19   Morriss 1983, 50.
20   Coad 1989, 225. I am grateful to Ann Coats for drawing my attention to the documentary evidence that indicates this system was indeed installed.
21   Coad 1989, 225.
22   Ibid, 226; NA, ADM 140/249, part 2, for an elevation drawing by Simon Goodrich.
23   Coad 1973, 21; Coad 1989, 199–200.
24   Coad 1973, 88–9.
25   Ashworth 1998, 66.

Chapter 2

1   NA, ADM 1/3525. His warrant formally dates from 25 March 1796. For fuller accounts of Bentham's life and career, see Ashworth 1998; Bentham 1862; Coad 1989, 29–35; Filipiuk 1997, ix–xvi; Morriss 1983, 46–53.
2   Ashworth 1998, 64–5.
3   De Madariaga 1993, 86.
4   Bentham 1852b, Goodrich's letter quoted on pp 270–1.
5   Richards 1872.
6   M Powis Bale 1880.
7   Filipiuk 1997, xvi–xviii.
8   Ibid.
9   Coad 1989, 30.
10   NMM, ADM Q 3320, 22.4.1795.
11   NMM, ADM Q 3320, 2.6.1795.
12   Ibid, 10.10.1795; NMM, POR A 40, 24.12.1796.
13   Wilkin 1999, 190.
14   Ibid, 93.
15   Holland 1971, 149–50.
16   Coad 1989, 90; Dietz 2002, 144.
17   Coad 1989, 96–7.
18   This is clearly shown on the 1761 dockyard plan – NA, ADM 140/555, parts 1 and 2. A plan of 1770 shows the routes of the culverts and drain to the harbour – NA, ADM 140/555, part 5.
19   Coad 1989, 101–3.
20   Rodger 2004, 379.
21   Coad 1989, 101–3; NMM, POR A 38, 4.2.1795.
22   Ibid. The Portsmouth set of dry and wet docks are rivalled only by the smaller and younger group at Karlskrona Naval Base in Sweden.
23   Coad 1989, 99–100; NA, ADM 1/3525, 10.9.1798.
24   Ibid, 21.12.1797.
25   Ibid.
26   Ibid.
27   Patent No. 1831 of 26.11.1791 and patent No.1951 of 23.4.1793. He had further patents relating to manufacturing processes and to civil engineering. There is a drawing of one of his original saws in the Bentham collection at UCL, box xcxvii, fol 24, and other saws drawn by Burr in the SML and more drawings in the NA in the ADM/140 series.
28   NA, ADM 1/3525, 21.12.1797.
29   GC, A 753, 29.11.1817.
30   Ibid, 5.4.1798.
31   NA, ADM 1/3526, 27.9.1801, gives more details of this system of water mains.
32   NMM, POR A 4, 26.9.1799.
33   NMM, ADM Q 3320, 19.4.1798.
34   NA, ADM 140/496. There is a detailed drawing in the GC (C 11). For an assessment of the engine, see

Farey 1827, 669. He made several engines for Coalbrookdale (Raistrick 1953, plate facing 176) and one for a London mustard-maker. In fact this pattern was used by other makers. Simon Goodrich noted two while on his travels in the winter of 1799. One was used as a winding engine on a canal, hauling tubs up a bank to a lime kiln, and another was on a canal barge driving paddle wheels. Both of these were atmospheric engines. GC, E 1, pp 27–8, 39. I am grateful to Tony Woolrich for drawing my attention to these other examples, all of which were developed independently.

35   GC, C 101.
36   NMM, POR A 43, 3.3.1800.
37   Coad 1989, 105, plate 82.
38   NA, ADM 1/3525, 29.10.1799.
39   NMM, ADM Q 3320, 7.2.1800.
40   Ibid, 17.2.1800.
41   NMM, POR A 43, 31.10.1800.
42   Drawing dated 30 May 1800 in the Boulton and Watt Collection, Birmingham City Archive PF 276-277-278-279-280-281-282.
43   NMM, POR A 43, 9.12.1800.
44   GC, A 54, 31.1.1801,
45   NMM, POR A 45, 5.2.1802, 10.8.1802.
46   Ibid, 15.4.1802, 22.4.1802.
47   A number of drawings of this engine and boiler house survive. One dated 26 March 1800 is in the NA, ADM 140/503 and 504. An undated version is in the GC, C 15 and C 17.
48   GC, C 110. It is just possible this drawing relates to the replacement copper boiler installed in 1817–18. See GC, Book B38, 10.1.1818.
49   GC, A 24, 6.4.1800.
50   GC, A 28, 29.4.1800.
51   NMM, LBK 54, fol 131, July 1808.
52   NA, ADM 1/3526, 25.1.1801.
53   Coad and Lewis 1982, 158, 171–2. A cast-iron quadrant that linked the horizontal drive shaft from the Portsmouth steam engine to the well pump was removed from the obsolete well-head in 1994 and is currently (2005) in the Block Mills.
54   GC, A 682a.
55   GC, A 628a, 5. The location of the well is shown on NA, ADM 140/555,

fol 17. From internal evidence, this dockyard plan must date from c1805. The site of the well lies under the modern office building east of the Great Basin.

56   NA, ADM 1/3526, 27.9.1801; NMM, POR A 44, 16.12.1801.
57   NMM, ADM B 203, 29.1.1802. Details of the various pipe lengths and diameters, plus the 6,000 wrought-iron screwbolts for connecting the pipes, are in NMM, ADM Q 3321, 21.3.1802.
58   GC, Book 14, 20.8.1806.

Chapter 3

1   NA, ADM 1/3525, 25.9.1799.
2   Coad 1989, 104. Although undated, evidence would suggest that Wyatt put forward this idea in 1793 when he was looking at converting the double dock at Portsmouth.
3   NA, ADM 1/3525, 25.9.1799, 26.9.1799.
4   NMM, ADM Q 3320, 25.10.1799; NA, ADM 1/3525, 10.4.1800.
5   NA, ADM 1/3525, 25.9.1799.
6   NMM, POR A 43, 26.4.1800; POR A 45, 15.4.1802, 26.6.1802; NA, ADM 1/3526, 11.8.1802. Bunce was certainly involved in 1802 when a number of the piers collapsed. See NMM, POR A 45, 26.6.1802. He died on 18 October 1802 (GC, A 8).
7   NMM, POR A 44–47, Extra Estimates.
8   NMM, POR A 43, 29.3.1800.
9   NA, ADM 1/3526, 11.8.1802. See also NMM, ADM B 205, 15.6.1802 and 17.6.1802 for further details.
10   NMM, POR A 45, Extra Estimates.
11   NMM, POR A 45, 15.4.1802, 22.4.1802.
12   NA, ADM 1/3526, 11.8.1802.
13   NA, ADM 174/16, 30.11.1761.
14   GC, Book 18, 22.3.1808. The tanks were sited on the flat roofs behind the parapets. As with the lower tanks, they were probably made of timber and lined with lead.
15   NMM, POR A 45, 22.4.1802.
16   The adaptations and alterations occasioned by the decisions to incorporate Brunel's block-making machinery are a further obstacle to our understanding of the purely Bentham Wood Mills. Power could

have been taken to the north range – as indeed happened later– by overhead line shafting. Bentham would have been aware of Rennie's use of this at the Albion Mills, and also Strutt's work in his Derbyshire textile mills.

17   GC, Book 34, 5.9.1815. Goodrich records a visit with Brunel during which they discussed the use of 'leather rope'.
18   NMM, POR A 45, 22.4.1802.
19   NMM, POR A 46, 16.6.1803.
20   McGowan 1999, 12.
21   GC, Book 6B,19.5.1804. Bentham saws also illustrated in Wilkin 1999, pp 183 and 184 and in the following NA documents – Reciprocating saw: NA, ADM 140/501, drawing of reciprocating saw, signed by S Bentham, 31 May 1803; Circular saw: NA ADM 140/502 part 1, drawing of a circular saw, signed by S Bentham, 31 May 1803; Joiners saws SML GC C 12a, 12b, 12c . In addition, there is in the NA online catalogue a ref ADM 140/502 part 2. This is probably the big drag saw, described in Rees, and mentioned elsewhere in this book; .
22   NMM, LBK 54, 9.11.1806.
23   SML, Joshua Field Collection Arch, Field 2/35 and 2/36, 22.8.1806.
24   GC, Book 12, 29.11.1805. This saw had a diameter of 6ft (1.83m).
25   NMM, LBK 54, pp 61 and 63, letters to Maudslay, 9.4.1807, 13.4.1807, 15.4.1807.
26   GC, Book 17, 30.1.1807. Goodrich gives a full description of the treatment process.
27   GC, Book 6B, 12.7.1804.
28   Gilbert 1965, 12, gives a good description of this process. Bentham developed wood-cutting saws for his brother's proposed Panopticon prison. He later proposed installing ssaws at the Redbridge yard, and the drawing in the Bentham collection at University College, London, probably represents this later set-up (drawing UC cxvii, 24). In Bentham's 1803 proposals for saws for the Wood Mill, the drawing (in the NA) for the vertical reciprocating saw at Portsmouth shows that the drive was by means of a shaft running

under the ceiling above it, but the account of it in Rees notes that it was operated by an underdrive. The account of the horizontal reciprocating saw in Rees notes that the drive ran under the ceiling. In Bentham's reciprocating saws the blades were tensioned in a substantial wooden frame which ran between vertical slides. His patent (No. 1951 of 1793) also describes guide wheels. In addition there was installed the swing saw, which enabled a small diameter circular saw to climb around a larger diameter log, cutting as it went. This remained in use at Portsmouth until it was transferred to the National Museum of Science and Industry, London.

The only Brunel-designed saws known to have been installed at Portsmouth as part of the equipment are the surviving vertical lignum vitae saw, a surviving corner saw and a horizontal cross-cutting saw for lignum vitae of which only a sketch of the saw-frame is known.

29 GC, Book 15, 17.9.1806.
30 GC, A 163, 3.10.1805. Although not entirely clear, the record suggests that at this stage there were two saws of each design.
31 GC, Book 14, 20.7.1806. In this entry Goodrich mentions three circular saws all designed by Bentham and that 'modifications only had been made by Brunel'.
32 Ibid, 14.6.1806.
33 GC, Book 6B, 14.7.1804.
34 GC, Book B38, Undated but almost certainly compiled in the first half of 1818.
35 GC, Book 26, 15.4.1811.
36 GC, Book 32, 29.7.1814.
37 GC, Book A375, 17.4.1812; Book A522, 17.8.1814. John Chainey, the treenail-mooter, had then been in his job 41 years and was working to a contract agreed on 19 August 1803. It is possible this contract had prevented the earlier introduction of the new machinery.

Chapter 4
1 Gilbert 1965, 2.
2 NMM, LBK 54, p 242.

3 Gilbert 1965, 5.
4 Coad 1989, 230; Gilbert 1965, 5; Skempton 2002, 90–1.
5 Beamish 1862, 56.
6 NA, ADM 1/3526, 14.4.1802. There is no doubt that Bentham did have an input into the machine designs since they incorporate a number of features described in his earlier patent No. 1951 of 1793. However, Bentham's contributions were more in the nature of detailed improvements to refine and improve the performance of individual machines. They included twisted blades to the rotary milling cutters in the coaking machine to remove cuttings (pp 18–25 of the printed version); the crown saw of the rounding machine (p 26); reciprocating chisels in the mortising machine (p 33) and the differential mechanism for turning the block shells in the shaping machine (p 42).
7 Beamish 1862, 61.
8 NMM, ADM Q 3321, 2.8.1802.
9 Gilbert 1965, 5–6. There is some debate as to the precise number of the block machines manufactured by Maudslay. The Oxford Dictionary of National Biography (2004) suggests that the total was 44.
10 Cantrell and Cookson 2002, 23.
11 NMM, ADM Q 3321, 13.8.1802.
12 Ashworth 1998, 72.
13 NMM, ADM Q 332, 7.6.1803; NA, ADM 1/3527, 7.6.1803. Both letters are from Brunel to Bentham, but have slightly varying lists of tools.
14 GC, Book 5, 22.5.1804.

Chapter 5
1 NA, ADM 1/3526, 14.4.1802.
2 GC, A 182.
3 Rees's Cyclopaedia, vol 17, part 2, pub 22.4.1811, article on horology: plates on wheel cutters and Rehe's cutter grinder.
4 Henderson 1966, 24–5.
5 These were brass and grooved, or fluted, longitudinally, and rotary milling cutters were used in some instances to machine the flutes. In other instances a fixed tool cut the flute as the machine moved the roller to and fro beneath it. These little machines were precursors of

the larger planing and milling machines used in engineering workshops.
6 GC, A 182, p 1.
7 The records of the Society of Arts have no knowledge of Samuel Rehe, but there was a John Rehe of the same address who died in the same month. Royal Society of Arts, pers comm to Tony Woolrich, October 2004.
8 Forward 1923, 1; Coad 1989, 31.
9 A P Woolrich, pers comm.
10 A P Woolrich, 'Goodrich, Simon' in Skempton 2002, p 261, and Oxford Dictionary of National Biography 2004; GC, E 1; GC, A 59, 65–7, 69–71.
11 The Metal Mills, which were demolished in 1851, were originally designed to reprocess copper sheathing for warship hulls. However, in 1805 an iron foundry was ordered to be built as part of the complex. GC, A 155, 30.7.1805. By 1813, the Metal Mills were rolling 6,700 sheets of copper a week (Evans 2004, 22, 114).
12 GC, A 182, passim.
13 NA, ADM 1/3526, 7.6.1803.
14 GC, A 147, 30.6.1805.
15 Ibid.
16 NA, ADM 1/3527, 30.7.1805. The Goodrich papers contain a number of letters to the London engineering firm of Lloyd and Ostell. Whether this is a continuation of the career of John Lloyd, millwright, is not known.
17 Because of the shortness of time that he actually worked under Goodrich, he does not appear in his journals, but there are a number of letters in the GC from and to Field about marine engines, and the replacement 30hp engine at the Block Mills in 1830. A P Woolrich, 'Field, Joshua' in Skempton 2002, p 226, and Oxford Dictionary of National Biography 2004.
18 No. 1812 of 1791. For Barker's mill see Dickinson 1939, 187.
19 This is not given in the list of English patents, so it is probably a Scottish one. Farey 1827, p 669. This was illustrated in the Journal of Natural Philosophy, Chemistry and the Arts, vol 2 [1798], p 231.

20 H S Torrens, 'Sadler, James' in *Oxford Dictionary of National Biography* 2004.

21 Collinge 1978, 128.

22 Ashworth 1998, 71.

23 Gilbert 1965, 6. This figure is difficult to verify.

24 NMM, ADM Q 3321, 2.8.1802.

25 GC, A 8, 18.10.1802.

26 NMM, ADM Q 3321, 3.12.1802.

27 Quoted in Beamish 1862, 80.

28 Gilbert 1965, 5–6.

29 Beamish 1862, 81.

30 NMM, POR A 46, 17.8.1803; NA, ADM 1/3526, 9.9.1803.

31 NMM, ADM Q 3322, 27.5.1803.

32 Ibid, 31.5.1805, 20.6.1805; Gilbert 1965, 5.

33 NMM, ADM B 211, 7.9.1803. Three different sizes of machines were built for the different sizes of blocks required by the navy. The first set of machines was something of a test-bed for the designs and the configurations of several were changed in the light of experience when the second and third sets were built. The information noted here is taken Farey's comments in Rees's, *Cyclopaedia*.

The first morticing machines completed were the intermediate sized one. On each, the motion of the chisel frame was communicated to it by a long working beam or lever, extending the whole length of the top of the machine. At one end, this lever was linked by a connecting rod to the chisel frame; at the other, it was fixed to pin, supported by the framing, forming its centre of motion. A connecting rod was joined to it in the middle of the beam; and the lower end of this was worked by a crank, formed in the middle of the main axis. The drive axis in this machine was at right angles to the direction adopted in the two later sizes of machines. This machine made 400 cuts per minute, a faster rate than the later ones.

In the first shaping machine fewer blocks were machined at a time, (Farey did not record the numbers). Each block was separately indexed round 90° to cut a new face by a notched plate and a detent. In the later machines, which held ten blocks, this indexing was done automatically *en masse* by the use of a kind of differential gear based on Bentham's ideas. (*See* Chapter 4, note 6).

The first scoring machine lacked the rotating table, so that each half block was machined at each pass of the cutter. Half of the cut was thus against the grain of the wood and ripped it up, so in the subsequent machines the revolving table was introduced to prevent this by making two cuts per side.

Brunel did not illustrate these early versions in his notebook, now in the National Maritime Museum. The models of the mortising and shaping machines in the museum are of the later pattern, and it is possible they were made to replace the models initially demonstrated to the Admiralty.

34 Morriss 1983, 51.

35 NMM, ADM Q 3322, 31.8.1804; Sainty 1975, 139.

36 NA, ADM 1/3527, 24.3.1805.

37 NMM, ADM Q 3322, 2.6.1803.

38 Ibid, 1.6.1803.

39 Beamish 1862, 91. The author also states that Brunel's saw could cope with logs up to 36in (914mm) in diameter.

40 During these years, Brunel lived in a terraced house in Britain Street, Portsea. The house was demolished in the 1960s. Clements 1970, 37. *See* Fig 5.2

41 GC, A 182, *passim*.

42 Coad 1989, 32.

43 NA, ADM 1/3527, 24.9.1805.

44 GC, Book 10, 24.9.1805.

45 Ibid.

46 NMM, ADM Q 3323, 28.9.1805.

47 GC, Book 10, 8.10.1805.

48 Ibid, 13.10.1805, 28.10.1805. The Whitmore referred to here is almost certainly William Whitmore (c1748–1816), engineer and ironfounder, of Dudmaston Hall, near Bridgnorth Shropshire (Skempton 2002, 777). Murray and Wood's engine works at Holbeck, Leeds, was probably Boulton and Watts's most serious competitor. In his diary Goodrich sometimes refers to this firm as Fenton, Murray & Co (ibid, 461–2).

49 GC, Book 12, 3.12.1805. In September 1806 'William Whitmore & Son of Birmingham' sent the Admiralty a bill for £6,526 16s 9½d for the steam engine and machinery for the Copper Mills as against Bentham's estimate in 1803 of £5,066 16s 8d. NMM, ADM Q 3323, 13.9.1806.

50 Ibid, 20.12.1805.

51 GC, Book 14, 27.5.1806, 1.8.1806, 19.8.1806, 22.8.1806.

52 GC, Book 17, 19.3.1807.

53 GC, Book 19, 18.7.1807, 28.9.1807. This diary has numerous references to these boiler problems. The references to salts may indicate the use of harbour water or may refer to brackish well water. The latter was a problem in parts of Portsmouth. The new deep well may have helped solve the problem.

54 GC, A 218, 22.8.1807.

55 GC, A 1348, 10.4.1828.

56 Dickinson 1939, 119–22.

57 Interestingly, it was the Fenton and Murray engine that needed to be replaced. The older Boulton and Watt engine soldiered on to 1837.

58 GC, Book 10, 15.8.1805.

59 Ibid, 2.9.1805.

60 Ibid, 25.9.1805.

61 Ibid, 15.10.1805, 16.10.1805.

62 GC, Book 14, 14.6.1806. By November 'having an account of the great inconvenience arising from the Block Manufactory from the position of our present circular saw', Brunel had the latter moved (NMM, LBK 54, 9.11.1806).

63 Ibid, 29.6.1806. This would have been at Brunel's house in Britain Street, Portsea.

64 Ibid, 8.8.1806.

65 Ibid, 12.8.1806.

66 GC, Book 16, 22.10.1806.

67 GC, Book 10, 2.9.1805.

68 GC, Book 17, 17.3.1807.

69 Clements 1970, 41–2; NA, ADM 1/3527, 17.9.1808.

70 GC, Book 10, 23.11.1805.

71 Beamish 1862, 81.

72 Ibid, 82.

73 Ibid, 83.

74 GC, A 134, 13.2.1805.

75 GC, Book 10, 2–7.9.1805.

76 See in particular Ashworth 1998.

77 For an earlier visit in 1803, see 'Memoranda made of a journey to the north in 1803 to visit Mr Grimshaw's ropery and to the west of England', GC, E 2, pp 16–21. A full account of the 1804 visit, 'Memorandum on a journey north to visit Mr Grimshaw's ropery', is in GC, D 10.

78 GC, Book 10, 9.11.1805. No drawings of these lamps have so far been found, but Farey, writing in Rees's *Cyclopaedia*, noted the lamp glasses were barrel-shaped and had spark-proof tops (Tony Woolrich, pers comm).

79 GC, Book 10, 14.11.1805; Book 14, 9.7.1806, 10.7.1806 and 23.7.1806. These lamps may have remained in use until gas lighting was installed much later in the 19th century – see NA, Works 41/415.

80 GC, Book 19, 24.11.1807.

Chapter 6

1 Morriss 1983, 52.

2 Ibid.

3 NMM, ADM Q 3322, 4.1.1803.

4 Ibid, 31.8.1804.

5 NMM, ADM Q 3323, 19.2.1805.

6 NMM, LBK 54, 6.11.1806.

7 GC, Book 19, 4.9.1807.

8 GC, A 219, 3.9.1807. GC Book 12, 22.11.1805 notes that Maudslay gave the composition of the alloy as 16 parts copper, 3 parts brass and 2 parts tin. It was thus a species of gun metal.

9 NMM, LBK 54, letter from Brunel to Goodrich, 4.10.1807. The reference to the engines having to be altered probably indicates that the block-machinery had to be reset to make use of whatever coaks were available. GC, A 219.

10 Gilbert 1965, 1.

11 This chapter owes much to Carolyn Cooper's pioneering article on operations in this building (Cooper 1981–2).

12 In 1806 Goodrich is wondering whether to install a boiler 'for boiling the shells of the blocks', as well as creating a louvred room on the roof of either the north or south range 'for drying the block shells'. The purpose of this operation is not explained and nothing seems to have come of the suggestion. GC, Book 12, 7.2.1806. For position of louvres see Goodrich's sketch in the notebook.

13 Gilbert 1965, 14–15.

14 Ibid, 12.

15 M I Brunel, 'Block Machinery', NMM library, catalogue #SPB 11.

16 Cooper 1981–2, 34.

17 Ibid, 35; NA, ADM 1/3527, 5.5.1806.

18 Cooper 1981–2, 35.

19 SML, 463/1–2 Rees.

20 GC, Book B38, undated, but from other evidence compiled in 1818.

21 GC, D12. Tony Woolrich has drawn my attention to an 1829 order for bevel drive shafts for the Block Mills and suggests these may have replaced the original transmission system with the one shown on the 1850 plan of the layout. GC, A 1450, 11.8.1829.

22 Cooper 1981–2 and 1984.

23 Rees 1812.

24 GC, Book 10, 30.8.1805.

25 Cossons 1993, 135.

26 Coad 1989, 233.

27 GC, Book 13, 13.5.1806.

28 GC, A 766, 15.1.1818; NA, ADM 140/63–5. The drawings for the new machines are in the NA ADM 140/637-51.

29 NMM, CHA R 2, 30.12.1815.

30 Coad 1989, 233, the sawmill still stands and contains a considerable quantity of early saw-frames.

31 GC, Book 6B, 19.5.1804. Cant timbers were the sharply angled parts of a bulkhead frame. Compare this list with that for 1854 on p 107–8.

32 NMM, ADM Q 3323, 19.2.1805.

33 Wilkin 1999, 116.

34 Morris notes that over the period 1805–13 the tonnage of new war-ships launched in the six main dock-yards almost doubled compared to the period 1793–1801. Construction times were also significantly reduced. Morris 1983, 30.

Chapter 7

1 GC, Book 10, 2.9.1805.

2 Beamish 1862, 89. Beamish says that he wrote to 'Commissioner Grey'; he may be mistaken. The Hon. Charles Grey (Viscount Howick) was not appointed First Lord until the following February. It seems more likely that Brunel wrote to Saxton at Portsmouth. In Jane Austen's *Mansfield Park* (chapter 41), visiting the dockyard was clearly a popular local pastime, during which 'the young people sat down upon some timber in the yard, or found a seat on board a vessel in the stocks'.

3 Beamish 1862, 89.

4 GC, Book 17, 31.1.1807.

5 Ibid, 17.2.1807.

6 GC, Book 22, 17.7.1810; Book 23, 18.10.1810.

7 GC, Book 32, 2.3.1814. This was confirmed by an Order in Council dated 21 April 1814. GC, A 519, 21.6.1814. Edward Holl was the civil architect.

8 GC, A 519, 21.6.1814.

9 GC, Book 32, 18.6.1814.

10 Filipiuk 1997, 11. The master of the Wood Mills was James Burr.

11 *The Times*, 27.6.1814.

12 Noble 1938, 24.

13 Ibid.

14 GC, Book 70, 28.10.1830. Goodrich was 57. The royal archivist advises that the princess kept no record of the visit (letter to Tony Woolrich, 16.11.2004).

15 Willis 1852, 311.

16 Bentham 1852b. This paper (and others M S Bentham had published earlier) discussed exhaustively the woodworking machinery her husband had developed and which had been introduced at Portsmouth and Plymouth.

17 Beamish 1862, chapter V.

18 These began to appear from 1811 and were written and illustrated by John Farey jun (1791–1851) who had gained a formidable reputation for the articles and drawings he had contributed to Rees's *Cyclopaedia* since 1805. He also worked as a patents specification draughtsman, which accounts for his detailed descriptive texts. The most important works were Brewster's *Edinburgh Encyclopaedia*, vol 3, c1811 (16,000

word account, with 5 plates); 'Manufacture of ships' blocks', Rees's *Cyclopaedia*, vol 22, 1812 (28,000 word account, with 7 plates); *Encyclopaedia Britannica*, supplement to 4th edn, 1824 (5,050 words, not illustrated) – this is not so technical as the former accounts, but it does include financial information about costs and profits not recorded elsewhere. Later encyclopaedic accounts all derive from these, and continued to appear well into the 19th century. All these articles rightly concentrated on the actual block-making machines, which were illustrated. Although the saws were mentioned in passing, they were not illustrated, thus unwittingly depriving Bentham of his due.

Chapter 8

1   GC, A 605, 10.8.1815.
2   GC, A 613, 20.10.1815. Holl, however, revised the design and replaced the circular upper parts of the chimneys by a square design. Goodrich noted in a comment in the margin of the letter 'this acted as a damper upon my volunteering anything'.
3   Evans 2004, 29. Woolwich initially was to be the premier steam dockyard. Its location close to the main engine and machinery manufacturers had obvious benefits.
4   Evans 2004, p 68, fig 59; pp 131–4.
5   NA, Works 41/415.
6   Evans 2004, 28.
7   Anon 1854.
8   Ibid.
9   Barlow 2002, 87. This is not a complete list of surviving equipment.
10   Portsmouth Royal Naval Museum, 'Register of the names of block mill workers', Accession No. 1359.
11   Ballard 1980, 250.
12   Brown 1997, 52–3. Their sail area in relation to their size was about half that of the all-timber sailing warships.
13   Archibald 1971, 46.
14   Riley 1976, 9.
15   *See* Evans 2004 for a full account, setting Portsmouth in its wider naval context.
16   Riley 1985, 27; Bugler 1966, 184–7.
17   Evans 2004, 16, has a good pre-First World War aerial photograph.
18   Barlow 2002, 88, and pers comm. After 1982 block-making was undertaken for a short time by the mast-house shipwrights in No. 4 Boathouse.
19   Gilbert 1965.
20   Guillery 2003.
21   This is unlikely to provide the whole picture as parts of the ground floor have been replaced by concrete.

Appendix

1   NA, Works 41/321.
2   GC, D 103–109.
3   GC, A 93.
4   GC, D 12.
5   Cooper 1981–2, figs 4, 5.
6   GC, Book 6B, fig F.
7   NMM, MS 184/149.

BIBLIOGRAPHY

Nineteenth-century encyclopaedias

Brewster, D c1811 *Edinburgh Encyclopaedia*, Vol 3
Encyclopaedia Britannica 1824, supplement to 4th, 5th and 6th edns, vol 2, part 2, 'Block-machinery', 337–41
Partington, C F 1835 The British Cyclopaedia of the Arts and Sciences ..., Vol 1 'Blocks', 217. London: Orr and Smith
Rees, A 1812 Cyclopaedia, Vol 22, 'Manufacture of ships' blocks'

General bibliography

Anon 1854 'A scheme of prices for performing work at the Wood Mills'. Portsmouth Royal Naval Museum
Archibald, E H H 1971 *The Metal Fighting Ship in the Royal Navy 1860–1970*. London: Blandford
Archibald, E H H 1972 *The Wooden Fighting Ship in the Royal Navy AD 897–1860*. London: Blandford
Ashworth, W J 1998 '"System of Terror": Samuel Bentham, accountability and dockyard reform during the Napoleonic Wars'. Social History **23**, 63–79
Bale, M Powis 1880 *Woodworking Machinery: its rise, progress and construction*. London: C Lockwood & Co (Reprinted Lakewood, Colorado USA, 1992)
Ballard, G A 1980 *The Black Battlefleet*. Lymington: Nautical Publishing
Barlow, A 2002 'The Blockmills at Portsmouth Dockyard in the eighteenth to twentieth century'. *Mariner's Mirror* **88**, 81–90
Beamish, R 1862 *Memoir of the Life of Sir Marc Isambard Brunel*. London: Longman, Green, Longman and Roberts
Bentham, M S 1852a 'Historical notice of the introduction of machinery into the English dockyards'. *Mechanics Magazine*, **1487**, 102–3
Bentham, M S 1852b 'The invention of wood-cutting machinery – Sir Samuel Bentham – Mr Brunel'. *Mechanics Magazine*, **1496**, 264–76
Bentham, M S 1862 *Life of Brigadier-General Sir Samuel Bentham, by His Widow, M.S.B.* London
Brown, D K 1997 *Warrior to Dreadnought: Warship Development 1860-1905*. London: Chatham Publishing
Bugler, A 1966 *H.M.S. Victory: Building, Restoration and Repair*. London: HMSO.
Burton, A 1975 *Remains of a Revolution*. London: Sphere Books
Cantrell, J and Cookson, G 2002 *Henry Maudslay and the Pioneers of the Machine Age*. Stroud: Tempus
Clements, P 1970 *Marc Isambard Brunel*. London: Longmans
Coad, J G 1973 'Two early attempts at fire-proofing in royal dockyards'. *Post-Medieval Archaeology* **7**, 88–90
Coad, J G 1981 'Historic architecture of H. M. Naval Base, Portsmouth, 1700–1850'. *Mariner's Mirror* **67**, 3–59.
Coad, J G 1983 'Historic architecture of H. M. Naval Base, Devonport, 1689–1850'. *Mariner's Mirror* **69**, 341–92
Coad, J G 1989 *The Royal Dockyards, 1690–1850*. Aldershot: Scolar Press
Coad, J G and Lewis P N 1982 'The later fortifications of Dover'. *Post-Medieval Archaeology* **16**, 141–200

Collinge, J M 1978. *Navy Board Officials, 1660–1832*. London: University of London
Cooper, C C 1981–2 'The production line at Portsmouth Block Mill'. *Industrial Archaeology Review* **6**, 28–44
Cooper, C C 1984 'The Portsmouth system of manufacture'. *Technology & Culture* **25**, 182–225
Cossons, N 1993 *The BP Book of Industrial Archaeology*. Newton Abbot: David & Charles
Crossley, A S 1961 'Simon Goodrich, his work as an engineer: part 3, 1813–23'. *Trans Newcomen Soc* **32**, 79–91
De Madariaga, I. de 1993 *Catherine the Great: A Short History*. New Haven: Yale University Press
Dickinson, H W 1939 *A Short History of the Steam Engine*. Cambridge: Cambridge University Press
Dietz, B 2002 'Dikes, dockheads and gates: English docks and sea power in the sixteenth and seventeenth centuries'. *Mariner's Mirror* **88**, 144–54
Evans, D 2004 *Building the Steam Navy*. London: Conway Maritime
Farey, J 1827 *A Treatise on the Steam Engine, Vol 1*. London (reprinted Newton Abbot: David & Charles, 1971)
Filipiuk, M (ed) 1997 *George Bentham: Autobiography, 1800–1834*. Toronto: University of Toronto Press
Forward, E A 1923 'Simon Goodrich and his work as an engineer: part 1, 1796–1805'. *Trans Newcomen Soc* **3**, 1–15
Forward, E A 1938 'Simon Goodrich and his work as an engineer: part 2, 1805–1812'. *Trans Newcomen Soc* **18**, 1–27 (for part 3, see under Crossley, above)
Gilbert, K R 1965 *The Portsmouth Blockmaking Machinery*. London: HMSO
Guillery, P 2003 *The Block Mills, Portsmouth Naval Dockyard, Hampshire: An Analysis of the Building*. English Heritage Report B/0 16/2003. Swindon
Henderson, W O 1966 *J. C. Fischer and his Diary of Industrial England*. London: Frank Cass
Holland, A J 1971 *Ships of British Oak: The Rise and Decline of Wooden Shipbuilding in Hampshire*. Newton Abbot: David & Charles
McGowan, A 1999 *HMS Victory: Her Construction, Career and Restoration*. London: Chatham Publishing
Morriss, R 1983 *The Royal Dockyards during the Revolutionary and Napoleonic Wars*. Leicester: Leicester University Press
Morriss, R 2004 *Naval Power and British Culture, 1760–1850*. Aldershot: Ashgate
Noble, C B 1938 *The Brunels, Father and Son*. London: Cobden Sanderson
Oman, C 1968 *Nelson*. London: Sphere Books
Oxford Dictionary of National Biography 2004. Oxford: Oxford University Press
Portsmouth Royal Naval Museum, 'Register of the names of block mill workers', Accession number 1359.
Raddall, T H 1993 *Halifax, Warden of the North*. Halifax: Nimbus Publishing
Raistrick, A 1953 *Dynasty of Iron Founders*. London: Longman
Raymond, B 1999 *Tracing the Built Form of H. M. C. Dockyard*. Halifax: Nova Scotia Department of Education and Culture

Richards, J 1872 *A Treatise on the Construction and Operation of Woodworking Machinery*. London

Riley, R C 1976 *The Industries of Portsmouth in the Nineteenth Century*. Portsmouth: Portsmouth City Museums

Riley, R C 1985 *The Evolution of the Docks and Industrial Buildings in Portsmouth Royal Dockyard, 1698–1914*. Portsmouth: Portsmouth City Museums

Rodger, N A M 1986 *The Wooden World: An Anatomy of the Georgian Navy*. London: Collins

Rodger, N A M 2004 *The Command of the Ocean: A Naval History of Britain, 1649–1815*. London: Allen Lane

Roland, H 1899 'The revolution in machine-shop practice'. *Engineering Magazine* [New York] **18**, 41–58

Sainty, J C 1975 *Admiralty Officials, 1660–1870*. London: Athlone Press

Semple, J 1993 *Bentham's Prison*. Oxford: Clarendon Press

Sims, W L 1985 *Two hundred years of history and evolution of woodworking machinery*. Burton Lazars, Leicestershire: Privately printed

Skempton, A W 2002 *A Biographical Dictionary of Civil Engineers in Great Britain and Ireland, Vol 1, 1500–1830*. London: Thomas Telford Publishing

Skempton, A W and Johnson, H R 1962 'The first iron frames' *Architectural Review*, March, 175–86, London (reprinted *in* R J M Sutherland, ed, 1977 *Structural Iron, 1750–1850* Aldershot: Ashgate)

Wilkin, F S 1999 'The application of emerging new technologies by Portsmouth Dockyard, 1790–1815'. Unpublished PhD thesis (Open University)

Willis, R 1852 'Machines and tools for working in metal, wood and other materials'. *Lectures on the Results of the Great Exhibition of 1851*. London: Society for the Encouragement of Arts, Manufactures and Commerce, 293–320

Primary sources

Samuel Bentham, Patent Nos 1838 of 1791 and 1951 of 1793. These were printed by the Commissioners of Patents in 1851. Page references in the text refer to this printed edition.

National Archives, Kew

National Maritime Museum, London
  Marc Isambard Brunel's letterbook, 1806–11: LBK 54
  Marc Isambard Brunel's block-machinery notebook: SPB 11

Science Museum Library, London
  Goodrich Collection (GC)
  A Papers, 1707–1847
  B Journals and Memorandums, books 1–78
  C Drawings
  D Printed material
  E Miscellaneous

INDEX

Page references in **bold** refer to illustrations.